THE NAMES OF JESUS

The Names of Jesus

A.B. Simpson

CHRISTIAN PUBLICATIONS
CAMP HILL, PENNSYLVANIA

Christian Publications
3825 Hartzdale Drive
Camp Hill, PA 17011
www.cpi-horizon.com

Faithful, biblical publishing since 1883

ISBN: 0-87509-844-4
Mass market edition

98 99 00 01 02   5 4 3 2 1

CONTENTS

The Wonderful Counselor

For to us a child is born,
to us a son is given,
and the government will be on his
shoulders.
And he will be called
Wonderful Counselor, Mighty God,
Everlasting Father, Prince of Peace.
(Isaiah 9:6)

The idea of a child king was not unfamiliar to the Old Testament. Little Samuel had been Israel's best prophet and judge; young Josiah, wearing a crown at the tender age of five, was the best of Judah's kings after David.

All these were types of Jesus, God's holy and anointed King. With beautiful simplicity, even after His resurrection and ascension, the apostles speak of Him in their prayers to the Father as "thy Holy Child, Jesus." He Himself has told us that His best representative on earth is a little child. "And whoever welcomes one of these little children in my name (that is, belonging to me) welcomes me" (Mark 9:37a). And even His Father in heaven is not ashamed to be represented by the same little child. "Whoever welcomes me does not welcome me but the one who sent me" (37b).

There is nothing more beautiful in an old and venerable man than the simplicity of childhood which often characterizes the greatest minds. Perhaps when we meet with our God, we will be touched most of all by the simplicity of His presence. At least, it is very beautiful to know that the Christ who comes still to guide and govern us is a child Christ, gentle as the touch of an infant's hand, accessible as your own little ones, easy to approach, simple and loving as an innocent child; yet mighty as the Mighty God and the Everlasting Father.

It is very touching to notice in the apocalypse that Jesus is continually described by a diminutive term of peculiar endearment; not the Lamb, as it is translated in our version, but literally "the little Lamb, the dear Lamb of God."

Let us look, however, at the other side of the picture, and, as we do, let us carry with us the concept of the child. Four illustrious and glorious names are here given to Jesus.

The Wonderful Counselor

This name has reference to His prophetic work and office, for He is our prophet as well as our King, the great teacher and guide to His people. The term "counselor" has reference to His guidance rather than to His teaching. One may know much and be able to say much, and yet not be a good counselor. Jesus is our wisdom and leads His trusting children in the right paths where they will not stumble.

1. He often leads us contrary to the ideas, opinions and judgments even of wise men, and His thoughts are as high above our thoughts as the heavens above the earth. If He is our guide, He will often bid us do things which prudence regards as folly, possibly as fanaticism; but God will vindicate His own wisdom in the end, and "wisdom is proved right by her actions" (Matthew 11:19b).

It must have seemed a very foolish thing to the Canaanites to have an army march seven days around their city walls and then simply blow their trumpets and shout, but it was the wisest way to take Jericho. It must have seemed a very foolish thing to ask a widow to give away her last handful of meal to a stranger when she and her boy were starving, but it was the best way to save her and her boy from starvation and to open the way for a continual supply for the coming months. It must have seemed an absurd thing for young David to face the giant Philistine with a simple sling and stones, but it was the only way by which he could have obtained the victory. It must have seemed absurd to commit to 12 fishermen the task of evangelizing the world, but it was God's wisdom, and it became God's mighty power. It may have appeared very strange to Philip for the divine message to come to him to leave Samaria in the height of his

great evangelistic work there and go down into a
lonely desert where he could not expect to meet a
soul, but it was God's way to preach the gospel to
the Prince of Ethiopia and, through him, to the
whole of Northern Africa. He leads us by a way that
we know not; but it is ever the right way, and we
will thank Him at last that He has proved our
Wonderful Counselor.

2. He is a Wonderful Counselor because the
people He leads are such weak and foolish people.
When we commit ourselves to the guidance of
Christ we become weaker in ourselves, ceasing to
look to our own wisdom. Without His guidance we
would indeed be utterly helpless, but this is our
very strength. The little child who knows nothing
of the way through the strange city is safer than
the one who knows a little. The latter is very apt to
trust in his or her imperfect knowledge and go
astray. But the former, knowing nothing, simply
holds his or her mother's hand and is safely led by
one who knows better. And so it is said of the
heavenly pathway:

> And a highway will be there;
>   it will be called the Way of Holiness.
> The unclean will not journey on it;
>   it will be for those who walk in that Way;
>   wicked fools will not go about on it.
>   (Isaiah 35:8)

"Not that we are competent," says Paul, "to claim
anything for ourselves, but our competence comes

from God" (2 Corinthians 3:5), and it is indeed wonderful how the most simple-hearted and un-educated minds are led by the Holy Spirit, not only into full knowledge of God's Word, but kept from error and mistake and guided safely through all the mazes of life's pathway!

His patience and love

3. This Counselor is wonderful in His patience and love. He is willing to take infinite trouble with us. Over and over again He teaches us the lessons we are so slow to learn. Over and over again He repairs our mistakes and lifts us up from our stumblings, saying to us, "How is it that you do not understand?"

There is no difficulty too intricate for Him to unravel. There is no little detail of life too petty for Him to take an interest in. There is no toil too tedious for Him to go through with us. There is no tangle too involved for Him to unthread and loose. There is no complication of difficult circumstances too extreme for Him to be willing to take hold of and lead us gently out into the light.

Even our stupidity and rebellion have not always provoked Him to leave us; but He waits, loves and leads us, until at last He brings us into His perfect will and our hearts are ready to say, "Wonderful Counselor, patient Teacher, gentle Christ—who teaches like Him?"

4. The best of all about this Wonderful Counselor is that He does not merely tell us what to do and give us a chart of the way, but He comes with

us every step of the way and becomes our personal
guide.

If you were to go to Cairo and try to find directions about the best way to cross the desert from
some Bedouin, or perhaps some map of the way or
some itinerary of stations, he would laugh at you
and say, "Why, you will never find your way in that
manner. I cannot tell you the way, but I will go
with you and show you the way. I will be your personal guide." This is exactly what Jesus does. He
says, "I am the way and the truth and the life"
(John 14:6a). He says that,

> When he has brought out all his own, he goes
> ahead of them, and his sheep follow him be-
> cause they know his voice. But they will never
> follow a stranger; in fact, they will run away
> from him because they do not recognize a
> stranger's voice. (10:4–5)

"The Counselor, the Holy Spirit" (14:26a) will "be
with you forever" (14:16b), and "he will guide you
into all truth" (16:13a).

Receiving guidance

How may we have the guidance of this Wonderful Counselor? First, it is always necessary that we
be wholly yielded to follow His guidance and have a
single purpose to please Him only. Willingness will
ever miss the way, but "he guides the humble (the
yielded ones, the little and bending hearts) in what
is right/ and teaches them his way" (Psalm 25:9).

Second, we must bring to Christ every particular need and acknowledge Him in all our ways, and He will direct our steps. It will not do to take it as a matter of course and say it will be all right anyhow, for the very thing in which we ignore Him is most likely to go wrong just because we have trusted in general and not specifically recognized Him.

Third, let us not expect startling revelations to come, but go by the simple light of His Word and our sanctified judgment and the voice of the Spirit as He speaks to us through quiet convictions, intuitions and impulses. There are voices and voices. There is light that will come to us all, but it is false light. It may often be known by its blaze and glare. God's light is the soft simple light that rests us and brings the satisfying sense of His presence and peace.

Last, if we have His light, let us be willing to take it step by step. We will not see all the way at once, but as we follow on we will know the Lord in all His fullness, and all His purposes will ripen and unfold in all their fullness.

The Mighty Fullness

He who is our Counselor is also abundantly able to carry out His plans, and He always follows up His directions with His strong and mighty hand. He never sends us on any path without standing by us and seeing us through. He who sent Israel around Jericho never fails to level the walls at the right moment. He who bid the people to go forward into the sea never fails to divide the floods.

He who sends us through the waters and the fires never fails to go before us and keep them from overflowing us. He who bids us march up against the gates of brass never fails to precede us and break in pieces the brazen gates and make the crooked places straight. When the Holy Spirit is working in us, the mighty providence of God is always working outside of us in perfect correspondence and preparation.

The Christ of the gospel is the Jehovah of the Old Testament—the God who said to Jeremiah, "Is anything too hard for me?" (32:27b). He is the God of creation and of providence—the God who said to Moses, "I lift my hand to heaven and declare:/ As surely as I live forever . . . and no one can deliver out of my hand" (Deuteronomy 32:40, 39).

He is able to control all the forces and elements of nature, able to restrain all the influences and movements of society, able to turn the hearts of men at His pleasure and overthrow their counsels and their works. He is able to save the lost, to pardon the guiltiest soul, to cleanse the blackest heart, to renew the most wrecked and ruined life. He is able to fill the heart of sorrow with untroubled gladness. He is able to take away the strongest tendencies to sin and give the degraded and selfish soul the power to do that which is right and holy. He is able to satisfy our inmost, utmost being. He is able to put His own heart and nature in the most corrupt and helpless soul. He is able to touch the springs of physical life and fill them with His own strength and healing. He is able to meet the temptations that overcome us and to make us more than conquerors in all things through His love. He is able to make even our little lives mighty forces for everlasting good, and so clothe us with His power that we will be able to open the blind eyes and turn men from darkness into light and from the very power of Satan to God. He is still standing among us and saying: "All authority in heaven and on earth has been given to me . . . Surely, I am with you always, to the very end of the age" (Matthew 28:18–20).

He is greater than the greatest difficulty, the greatest sin, the greatest sorrow, the greatest failure in your life. From this day place Him, your mighty God, over against the things that are too strong and too hard for you. Only touch the hand of the little Child, and lo, all the forces of Omnipotence, if need be, will be called forth to blast the very rocks of adamant, to roll back the tides of the ocean, to prepare the way for His ransomed.

> When He makes bare His arm,
> Who shall His power withstand?
> When He His people's cause defends,
> Who, who shall stay His hand?

The Father of Eternity

This is the true translation of this strange verse. It means that His being is unlimited, His years eternal, His element boundless and all His plans and thoughts shaped and drawn on a gigantic and infinite scale. Eternity begins for us before time ends. The life we have now is eternal life. It takes hold upon illimitable things. There is about it a depth and a height, a length and a breadth that defy all calculations and computations, and the things that we take from God and do for God are eternal things. We now see but a little of what will be revealed, but when He appears we will be like Him.

Let us build today for eternity. Let all our thoughts, plans and hopes be in view of the gigantic future, the colossal scale that is to unfold when we pass into the illimitable beyond. Let us ever see ourselves as we will be then and our work as it will seem then. Let us be content with nothing that is not going to last. Let us, like Him, belong to the ages to come.

Ours is not an ephemeral breath of life, like the fluttering moth or butterfly, like the flashing meteor of the sky. We will live when the sun is burned to ashes and the stars have faded away or taken on their new and everlasting forms.

Could we see today the scope of our future being, the height of our future glory, the grandeur of our future reward, we would be afraid. We would be paralyzed with awe and then with shame at the pettiness of our conceptions of God and our expectations from Him.

Let us give our future to Him who is the Father of Eternity. Let us lay up our treasures in hands that will give them back there with the compound interest of their glory. Let us take more of the vastness, rise to more of the boundlessness of thought and purpose, of love and faith, of joy and service, which He expects of those who would be worthy of His great and infinite heart that throbs within us.

The Prince of Peace

There is an allusion here to the kingdom of Solomon, whose name was significant of peace and whose reign was typical of the coming King, his greater Son. It is to Him that the 72nd Psalm is dedicated, with its beautiful words, "Let the mountains bring peace to the people,/ And the hills, in righteousness. . . . In his days may the righteous flourish,/ And abundance of peace till the moon is no more" (verses 3, 7, NAS).

His first conquest is through the gospel of peace. Having made peace through the blood of the cross, He came to preach peace to all. His coming was heralded with the words, "on earth, peace to men on whom his favor rests" (Luke 2:14b). His last bequest before He died was, "Peace I leave with you; my peace I give you" (John 14:27a). His benediction as He arose and met them in the upper room was, "Peace be with you" (John 20:19b). "Since we have been justified through faith, we have peace with God through our Lord Jesus Christ" (Romans 5:1).

He brings to the guilty heart the sense of pardon and eternal peace. Then He brings to the surrendered heart the deeper rest that comes from passion and sin subdued and perfect trust in Him as the sovereign and keeper of the soul. He brings peace by conquest, but His conquest is that of love, the soul subdued into harmony with Him by its own consent, and every part of the being in harmony with itself.

His glorious kingdom of peace extends further, for it brings us into perfect harmony with all the relations of life and circumstances that surround us. The soul in which this glorious Prince reigns easily adjusts itself to every situation. It finds God adjusting everything in its life in glorious rest and fitness, so that it is true that "when a man's ways are pleasing to the LORD,/ he makes even his enemies live at peace with him" (Proverbs 16:7). And where things are at war with us, we have a still higher victory. Then we can cry, with Paul,

> We know that in all things God works for the good of those who love him, who have been called according to his purpose. (Romans 8:28)

> I have learned to be content whatever the circumstances. I know what it is to be in need, and I know what it is to have plenty. I have learned the secret of being content in any and every situation, whether well fed or hungry, whether living in plenty or in want. I can do everything through him who gives me strength. (Philippians 4:11b–13)

And so the government will be on His shoulders; and when it is, it is true that "of the increase of his government and peace there will be no end" (Isaiah

9:7a). They that fully trust Him will find Him able to carry on His shoulder, not only the government of their own life, but all the things that concern them.

Wonderful names! Wonderful Savior, Counselor and Prince! Let us give Him the increase of the government and enter into His perfect peace. Then in a little while we will find ourselves in the glorious millennial kingdom of His everlasting peace. There the last enemy will be destroyed and universal nature will at length be brought into perfect and everlasting accord with His love and will. War will cease and strife will disappear. Sin will come no more, and sorrow will have passed away. Satan will be cast out; storms will never darken its sunny skies. Universal peace and everlasting love, like a golden chain, will bind the heavens and the earth together in one long endless kingdom of felicity and peace.

The Rock of Ages

*You will keep in perfect peace
    him whose mind is steadfast,
    because he trusts in you.
Trust in the Lord forever,
    for the Lord, the Lord, is the Rock eternal [Rock of Ages, KJV]. (Isaiah 26:3–4)*

The literal translation of this beautiful verse, as it will be found in the margin of our English Bible is, "The Lord JEHOVAH is the Rock of Ages." This is the foundation of that beautiful hymn which is one of the favorites of English-speaking Christians in the world: a hymn without which any collection would be absolutely incomplete. The imagery is very familiar to every Bible reader; rocks and mountains are associated with every important incident and epoch in the Bible.

- On Ararat the new world began.
- On Moriah the faith of Abraham was perfected.
- On Sinai the law was given.

- On Horeb the Tabernacle was designed.
- On Nebo the Land of Promise was unveiled.
- On Zion the capital of Judah was fixed.
- On Moriah the temple was reared.
- On Carmel the nation of Israel was called to their covenant God.
- On Mount Hattin Jesus preached His sermon.
- On Hermon He was transfigured.
- On Calvary He died.
- On Olivet He ascended.

It is not strange, therefore, that the mountain and the rock have become favorite expressions of sacred things for which their natural defenses, their immutable and changeless features, their colossal strength, their lofty eminence, their wide-reaching prospects of vision and their beauty so specially fit them.

The metaphor is repeated over and over again. "The Lord is our rock." "The rock of our heart." "The rock of our salvation." "The rock that is higher than we." "The shadow of a great rock in a weary land"; and here, sublimest of them all, "The Rock of Ages." This is the only passage in the Scriptures where this particular phrase, so full of deep meaning and majesty, is found.

Like some sublime mountain face, this text is a mighty and isolated rock in which we can trace the face of Jesus, our Rock of Ages. As we sit down under its mighty shadow, as we rest upon its velvet slopes, as we drink from the crystal fountains that flow from its side, we hear the sweet echo of our text: "You will keep in perfect peace/ him whose mind is steadfast,/ because he trusts in you./ Trust in the Lord forever,/ for the Lord, the Lord, is the Rock eternal."

The Rock

Higher even than its fine natural suggestiveness is the perfect Scriptural significance of this verse. It looks back to some of the most instructive and striking types of the Old Testament.

1. It recalls the rock in Horeb and speaks of Christ as our Savior. "I do not want you to be ignorant of the fact," says the apostle, addressing us New Testament Christians, "that our forefathers . . . all ate the same spiritual food and drank the same spiritual drink; for they drank from the spiritual rock that accompanied them, and that rock was Christ" (1 Corinthians 10:1–4). Perishing with thirst, the Israelites were led by Moses to the face of the rock in Horeb. Then the lawgiver lifted up his rod and smote the rock at God's command upon its naked face. Immediately it burst open, and from the cleft there poured a living stream, running through the camp in rivulets and floods of living water, until the thirsty thousands drank, and drank again, and gave their children and their cattle to drink until their thirst was fully satisfied. And they praised God for His great deliverance.

This incident has been applied with full Scriptural authority to the crucifixion of the Savior. He, for us, was smitten by the rod of the Lawgiver and Judge as our sacrifice and substitute, and from His pierced side there flows for us the water of life, where we can drink of His boundless mercies, His forgiving love, His renewing grace and thankfully sing,

> Rock in Horeb, riven for me
>   By the law's avenging rod,
> Flowing from thy side I see
>   Streams of water and of blood.
> And I wash my crimson soul
>   Whiter than the wool and snow,
> While the cleansing waters roll,
>   And the living fountains flow.

2. The Rock of Ages reminds us of the rock in Kadesh: the type of Christ, a fuller and more perfect Savior. Forty years after the rock of Horeb was smitten, the camp of Israel came to Kadesh. The old story was repeated again. Thirsty and hungry they murmured instead of praying, and once again their lawgiver led them to the rock. This time the command was different. He was not to smite the rock as before, but simply to speak to it, and the promise was given that the water should immediately gush forth.

In a moment of haste and disobedience, he exceeded his orders and smote the rock repeatedly with words of irritation, perhaps of unbelief. God honored His promise by sending the water abundantly again, but He was grieved with His servant for disobeying the explicit command; and for this offense Moses was excluded from the promised land. The waters, however, came forth, and the people drank abundantly, and the river continued to flow through the desert.

This is the type of the deeper fullness of Christ our Savior, and of the infinite grace of the Holy Spirit, which is simply waiting the call of faith on the part of every believer. This is not the atonement which first opened the rock of salvation for us; but this is the deeper fullness of the Holy Spirit, sanctifying and satisfying the soul.

The word "Kadesh" means righteousness, or holiness, and so this is the type of Christ our Sanctifier and Satisfier. This does not teach us of the Holy Spirit procured and sent down from heaven through the finished work of Christ, but the Holy Spirit already given and simply waiting the call of faith to be received.

We do not need now to smite the rock, to crucify Christ again, or to go through a desperate struggle and strain. We need simply to look and live, to take and have, to speak the simple words of trust, "Come, Holy Spirit, Heavenly Dove," and He answers quickly to our cry, and our prayer is changed to the song of praise:

> Rock of Kadesh, flowing still,
> From the Saviour glorified;
> All my empty being fill
> With thy Pentecostal tide.

The Following Rock

3. The Rock of Ages looks back to another

beautiful picture: "They drank from the spiritual rock that accompanied [followed, KJV] them" (1 Corinthians 10:4a).

What can this mean? "Following rock." Not that the rock moved through the desert, but the river that ran from the rock followed them through the desert. The rock followed them with its floods of life and cleansing.

The Psalmist tells us that when once in the desert they were perishing for want of water, they simply gathered in a little circle upon the burning sands and with their staves dug a little well in the sand, and lifted up their voices to God in songs of praise. Immediately the waters sprang up from the depths below and overflowed again, as at Horeb and Kadesh, from the subterranean springs.

So the Rock of Ages sends its living fountains all along our way and although the desert may be all around us and the wells may all seem dry, yet faith has only to make room and lift up the song of praise even in the hottest desert, and immediately the waters will spring forth in abundance, and we shall sing again:

> Following rock, from day to day,
>   Sending forth on every hand
> Rivers all along the way,
>   Underneath the desert sand.
> Open deep the living well,
>   Where Thy hidden fountains flow;
> Ever near Thee let me dwell,
>   As I through the desert go.

The Sheltering Rock

4. The Rock of Ages is also a sheltering rock. This is the rock of which the Psalmist cried, "Lead me to the rock that is higher than I" (61:2b). He shall be as "the shadow of a great rock in a thirsty land" (Isaiah 32:2b). A little rock only reflects upon us the more intensely the heat which it has absorbed; but the great rock drinks in the warm rays in one side, and on the other has a cooling shadow for the traveler who rests under its overshadowing cliffs. So, weak and selfish hearts only irritate us and throw over us the reflection of their burdens; but Christ is the shadow of a great rock. Occupied every moment as He is with the cares of others, with the sorrows of a weeping world, with the myriad prayers that are every moment surging into His ears, with the dying cries and groans of sinking souls, with the despairing shrieks of the wretched ones that are every moment drifting into eternity, He is always at leisure for us. He is always at our call. His whole heart is ever ready to comfort and rest us, as though there were not others in the wide universe but us requiring His sympathy and rest. Oh, the delightful peace, the safe refuge, the perfect security they enjoy who have found their home within the cleft of the Rock of Ages!

> Shadowing rock in weary lands,
>   Let me rest beneath Thy shade;
> Traveling o'er the burning sands,
>   Shelter my defenseless head.

Covert from the tempest rude,
  Refuge from the raging tide,
Fortress when by foes pursued,
  Let me in Thy bosom hide.

The Foundation Rock

5. The Rock of Ages is also a foundation rock. It is a place to build upon. It is the resting place of faith and hope. There trust finds its full assurance as it leans upon the promise, "Whoever believes in the Son has eternal life" (John 3:36a). There the soul can struggle with self and sin as it reposes all its weight upon the everlasting promise, "The blood of Jesus, his Son, purifies us from all sin" (1 John 1:7b). There hope anchors all her cables as she commits all her destinies, her affections and her treasures to this immovable rock and cries, "I know whom I have believed, and am convinced that he is able to guard what I have entrusted to him for that day" (2 Timothy 1:12b).

The mountains will depart and the hills will be removed, but this rock will stand. Our most substantial edifices will crumble into dust; our oldest institutions will vanish away; our securities and investments will be ashes in the flames of a dissolving world; but the Rock of Ages will remain unshaken and immovable, and, standing upon it amid the awful roar of the last great convulsion, we shall indeed be able to say,

God is our refuge and strength,

an ever-present help in trouble.
Therefore we will not fear, though the
earth give way
and the mountains fall into the heart of the
sea,
though its waters roar and foam
and the mountains quake with their
surging.

. . .

God is within her, she will not fall;
God will help her at the break of day.
(Psalm 46:1–5)

Rock of Ages, fixed and sure,
Be my faith's foundation stone;
Hopes we built on Thee endure,
Stable as Thy steadfast throne.
While my heart on Thee is stayed,
Winds may howl and torrents pour;
I shall never be afraid,
I am safe forevermore.

Such are some of the scriptural suggestions of
this beautiful name. There are further depths of
significance in it that no words can fully unfold. It
recalls to us not only the past associations of the
Bible, but the past associations of the people of the
church of God and our own experience. It is the
rock of the past. How touching it is to travel in
Bible lands and, as you sit down at the well of
Nazareth or Bethlehem, to think of the thousands
who in every generation have drunk of that foun-

tain and rested at that well! There Abraham rested
and drank. There Jesus came as a little child with
His mother. There crusaders, pilgrims, and great
travelers have quenched their thirst. How touching, how wonderful! It is the well of ages. This is
the Rock of Ages.

How it quickens one's pulse and moistens one's
eyes to go through the Tower of London and read
upon the walls the last messages of saints and mar-
tyrs—the verse of Scripture which they were lean-
ing their heads upon in view of the scaffold or the
stake upon the morrow! How wonderful to take
that 23rd Psalm and trace its record as it has been
written, not only in Bibles and letters bathed in
love and the prayers of human hearts and heavenly
anointing, but as it has been written on prison
walls and dungeon floors! Oh, how awesome one
feels, as he reads its verses, that he is treading on
sacred ground, and that every syllable is marked
with the footprints of some sufferer or victor that
has gone before!

And so, this Christ to whom we come has been
the Rock of Ages. The comfort He gives us has
been proved often before. He is "a tested stone,/ a
precious cornerstone for a sure foundation;/ the
one who trusts will never be dismayed" (Isaiah
28:16). He had been proved in temptation, in sick-
ness, in sorrow, in death. Other generations have
proved Him. Our fathers and mothers have proved
Him. Our past trials have proved Him.

Jesus, Jesus, how I trust Him,

How I've proved Him o'er and o'er,
Jesus, Jesus, precious Jesus,
    Oh, for grace to trust Him more!

And, as the Rock of Ages, He will live through future ages. He covers all the future, and He is keeping all that can ever concern us forevermore. Oh, let us trust in the Lord JEHOVAH forever: for the Lord JEHOVAH is the Rock of Ages.

The Rest

"You will keep in perfect peace/ him whose mind is steadfast [stayed, KJV],/ because he trusts in you./ Trust in the Lord forever" (Isaiah 26:3–4).

This blessed Rock is our place of rest. It is a place of perfect rest. "Peace! Peace!" is the marginal and more beautiful translation of this picture of the Christian's rest. There is a double peace. There is the peace of conscience that comes with justification and the deeper rest of God that comes with His indwelling, and the best of this is that He keeps it. It is a peace that abides forever and that keeps the heart in which it reigns: "And the peace of God, which transcends all understanding, will guard your hearts and your minds in Christ Jesus" (Philippians 4:7).

But there are conditions on our part. The first is *trust*. This is the sweet Old Testament word for faith—its child phase. It is not so much the intellectual act of believing as the heart attitude of confiding and trusting.

The next condition is *staying*. We not only trust,

but we stay trusting. There is a passive rest which is the result of indolence and inaction. It is simply drifting. The Christian's rest is an active reliance on the loving and everlasting arms of God. This will illustrate it. Look at a boat running before the breeze. Let that helm go lax, and the sails flap in the winds and the boat drifts and tosses with the tide, dashed about at the mercy of the billows, without any fixed course or steady poise. This is the attitude of many a life—simply drifting, trustless, restless, tempest-tossed and tending nowhere but to deeper unrest forevermore. But look at that boat now, as the experienced seaman sits down at the stern and puts his strong and steady hand upon the helm, pressing hard against the wind. See how the sails quickly fill and lean against the wind, like white-winged birds upon the air. Notice how the tossing vessel rights up and sets her prow against the waves in a steady course. Observe how the driftings and tossings cease, and the pitch and poise of the little ship are like the movements of a thing of life. Notice how swiftly she cuts her way through the raging waters, obedient to the joint impulse of the sail above and the helm astern. Notice how the very winds that almost cross her path, or blow in her very face, help her on her course.

That is a beautiful picture of the soul that is stayed upon God! The pressure of His providence, the very difficulties that confront us but quicken our steadfast trust we meet with the firm hand and fixed will of humble, holy confidence in God. How the will springs into steadiness and power! How its tossings are stilled, and its whole movement is quieted, intensely alive and active, yet intensely restful! It presses on, like that noble little ship, through wind and tide, in the will of God and the work of life. This is the picture of a soul stayed upon God.

The mind stayed on God

There is, further, a distinct reference here to the thoughts of the mind and their bearing upon the spirit of trust. It is the mind that is stayed upon God. Just translate this word "stayed" as "stopped," and carry with you the idea of a suspending of your busy thoughts, cares and activities, and you will understand better the prophet's meaning. The rest of faith is usually hindered most by the restlessness of our ever busy thoughts. We get to reasoning, questioning, wondering, fearing, looking forward to this emergency and that contingency, and our soul is disquieted by a whirlwind of conflicting thoughts. God wants us to stop thinking.

A lady came to spend a week or two in our home to learn the secret of our deeper life in Christ. Her face was clouded with care and her heart was distracted with doubts, anxiety and fears. She was really in danger of losing her mind through spiritual unrest. She came to our Friday meeting to be anointed for healing of this terrible pressure upon her mind. As we knelt by her side, we asked her if she would promise the Lord to stop thinking for a week. She said she could not, that at every instant she was like one swept by a hurricane of troubled thoughts. We told her she would and she must, that she needed to set her will firmly in the strength of God—like the ill birds that might beat their wings upon the window pane, she need not open the window and let them in; like the wild billows that might surge against the ship, and even flood the deck, she need not open the hatches and let them down into the cabin. She could simply stand guard at the door of her mind and refuse to receive these thoughts, to dwell upon them, to harbor them, to enter into sympathy with them. She could simply say, "I won't think," and as surely as she would do this and hold steadily to this attitude, the habit would soon become established, and her thoughts would be controlled. "But," she said, "shall I give up my good thoughts?" "Yes," our answer was, "everything at present, for all are unrestful. Even your good thoughts are evil, and when God gets you fixed in the habit of stillness, then He will breathe into you His thoughts without an effort upon your part."

At length she reluctantly consented to make the promise and set her will like a flint, in the name of the Lord, against all thinking and promised to learn to be perfectly still. Before the week had passed, her whole face and heart were perfectly transfigured. "The peace of God, which transcends all understanding" had taken possession of her soul, and she was rejoicing in the Lord and testifying to His victorious keeping grace and power.

You need to stay your heart on God; not on

thoughts or feelings, but on that Presence that will possess you utterly, and fill you with that peace "which transcends all understanding," as you turn away from all else to Him alone.

> Trust and rest in Christ forever,
>   Lean thy head upon His breast;
> Nothing from His love can sever
>   Those who simply trust and rest.
>
> Trust and rest in hours of sorrow;
>   Every wrong shall be redressed,
> In some happy, bright tomorrow,
>   If you only trust and rest.
>
> Trust and rest when all around thee
>   Puts thy faith to sorest test;
> Let no fear nor foe confound thee,
>   Wait for God and trust and rest.
>
> Trust and rest with heart abiding,
>   Like a birdling in its nest,
> Underneath His feathers hiding;
>   Fold thy wings and trust and rest.
>
> Trust and rest till gentle fingers
>   Fold thy hands across thy breast,
> While the echo softly lingers,
>   Everlasting trust and rest.

The First and the Last

I am the Alpha and the Omega, the First and the Last, the Beginning and the End. (Revelation 22:13).

As we think of the friends of life, how few there are that were linked with our earliest associations and memories! There was a period when every friendship began, and many of those we love the best we only knew for the first time a little while ago. But here a Friend addresses us who was before all other friends, who loved us long before we knew the love of brother, or even mother; long before we were even conscious of our own existence. "The Lord appeared to us in the past, saying: 'I have loved you with an everlasting love'" (Jeremiah 31:3a). Jesus is indeed the First.

And then, how many of those that were the first in our life are not the last? The very mother, on whose sweet face our eyes gazed before they recognized any earthly countenance, has long since passed from our view. Only a few of the friends of

youth remain, and how many of the fondest attach-
ments of life have been like rivers that run into the
desert and are lost amid the sands. But here we
have One who will be there at the close, who will
remain when all others have passed away, for Jesus
is the Last.

Amid the passing years and the passing forms of
loved ones and the changing scenes of life, how
sweet it is to know that Jesus is the First and the
Last! Let us gather up by the help of the Holy
Ghost some of the precious lessons of this wonderful name that covers all the present and the future.

The First

His preexistence

1. This expresses the eternal preexistence of
Christ. We find Him constantly declaring this in
His own addresses in the Gospel of John. "He was
before me" (John 1:30b) is the witness of John to
Him. "I came from the Father and entered the
world" (John 16:28a) is His own testimony. "Before
Abraham was born, I am" (John 8:58b). Even in the
Old Testament we have some sublime pictures of
the eternal Christ. "He will be called . . . Everlast-
ing Father (or the Father of Eternity)" (9:6b) is
Isaiah's picture. "Whose origins are from of old,/
from ancient times" (5:2) is Micah's picture.

> The Lord brought me forth as the first of his
>   works,
>   before his deeds of old;

I was appointed from eternity,
   from the beginning, before the world
     began.
When there were no oceans, I was given
     birth,
   when there were no springs abounding
     with water;
before the mountains were settled in place,
   before the hills, I was given birth,
      . . .
I was there when he set the heavens in place,
   when he marked out the horizon on the
     face of the deep,
      . . .
   Then I was the craftsman at his side.
I was filled with delight day after day,
   rejoicing always in his presence,
rejoicing in his whole world
   and delighting in mankind.
         (Proverbs 8:22–31)

This is Solomon's inspired picture of the eternal
Logos, His ancient love to the world and the men
that He was coming in the fullness of the ages to
redeem.

His preeminence

2. This expresses His preeminence. This also is
most clearly taught by the Holy Ghost in the Scriptures and claimed by Christ Himself. "That in
everything he might have the supremacy
[preeminence, KJV]" (Colossians 1:18b) is the

Father's purpose regarding His dear Son, for His is
the preeminence of deity. He is higher than all
men, higher than all angels, very God of very God,
the brightness of the Father's glory, the express
image of His person, the King of kings and Lord of
lords. There is no doubt that this is what He
claimed Himself, and for this claim His life was
threatened again and again by the Jews, and taken
at last in His final judgment and crucifixion. "He
must die, because he claimed to be the Son of God"
(John 19:7b) was their charge.

The hands into which we commit our souls are
divine and infinite hands. The ransom which has
been paid for our sin is of the infinite value of
deity. The grace that is sufficient for our full salvation is the grace of the infinite God. The kinship to
which He has raised us is nothing less than to be
partakers of the divine nature and sons and heirs of
God and joint heirs with Christ. Let us not fear to
bring forth every diadem and crown Him Lord of
all.

The work of creation and providence

3. This expresses His relation to the work of
creation and providence. This thought is expressed
by the Apostle Paul in his epistle to the Colossians
in these strong and significant words: "For by him
all things were created: things in heaven and on
earth, visible and invisible, whether thrones or
powers or rulers or authorities; all things were
created by him and for him. He is before all things,
and in him all things hold together" (1:16–17).

This expresses Christ's relation to the natural creation and to the affairs of providence. It was through His hand that the material universe was framed, and it is by His constant superintendence that the whole machinery of providence is carried on. By Him all things consist or, literally, "hang together." He is the cohesive force that holds the whole universe in order and harmony. All power is given to Him in heaven and in earth. Like the Roman centurion, all beings and forces are at the service of His will, and He can say to this one, "Go," and he goes, or to this one, "Come," and he comes, and to all things, "Do this," and they do it.

To Him we ascribe all the sublime descriptions that Jehovah gives us in the Old Testament of His sovereign power and glory. Every robe of majesty and might will fit the Son of God as perfectly as the Father, for it is He that does according to His will in the armies of heaven and among the inhabitants of the earth, and none can stop His hand from working, or say, "What are you doing?" In the midst of the throne ever sits the enthroned Lamb, while all angels and all creation sing in adoring reverence and love,

> Worthy is the Lamb, who was slain,
> to receive power and wealth and wisdom and
>   strength
> and honor and glory and praise!
> . . . .
> To him who sits on the throne and to the
>   Lamb

be praise and honor and glory and power,
        for ever and ever! (Revelation 5:12–13)

This is our Christ: the first and the last.

His relation to the Bible

4. This expresses also His relation to the Bible.
Christ is first in these sacred pages. The one object
of the Holy Scriptures is to reveal the person and
portrait of Jesus. This is the key to its interpretation; this is the glory of its pages—Jesus in the
story of creation, already planning the new creation; Jesus supreme above the ruins of the fall;
Jesus in the ark, the rainbow and the dove; Jesus in
the sacrifice on Mount Moriah, the ladder of Jacob
and the story of Joseph; Jesus in the Paschal lamb,
the desert manna, the smitten rock, the smoking
sacrifice, the fragrant incense, the suffering
scapegoat, the enrobed priest, the golden candlestick, the sacred ark, the sprinkled mercy seat, the
hovering cherubim, the awful Shekinah, the
glorious tabernacle and all its ministries and furniture; Jesus in the land of promise, in the temple of
Solomon, in the story of Joshua, the Psalm of
David, the throne of Solomon, the visions of Isaiah
and the panorama of ancient prophecy as it unfolds
toward the advent, the manger, the cross and the
throne; Jesus in the apostles; Jesus in the
apocalypse.

The testimony of Jesus is the Spirit of prophecy.
The face of Jesus can be traced like water lines in
fine paper back of every page, for He is the Alpha

and the Omega: the first and the last of this Holy Book.

His relation to redemption

5. This expresses the relation of Jesus Christ to redemption. He is the first in the plan of salvation. Long ago He was heard exclaiming, "I have come . . . I desire to do your will, O my God" (Psalm 40:7–8a). It has all been accomplished through Him, and His glory is all to return to Him, and He is forevermore to stand as the center and head of God's grandest work—the restoration of a ruined race, the salvation of sinful men. Christ is not only first in redemption: He is all. This winepress He hath trodden alone; none can share with Him this glory. His was all the cost; His alone the honor shall ever be. No name is so sublime in heaven as the Lamb, no song so loud as that which celebrates His redeeming love, and therefore all who receive this great redemption must give Jesus the supreme glory, or they cannot share it.

Relation to individual salvation

6. This expresses His relation to our individual salvation, for every soul must acknowledge Jesus as the first. "You did not choose me, but I chose you" (John 15:16a), He tells us. The first desire to come to Him came from Him. The very hunger that longed for Him was His grace beginning to enter our hearts. He has loved us with an everlasting love and, therefore, with loving-kindness has He drawn us. Not only has He pardon for us when we

repent, but He is exalted to give repentance to Israel and the remission of their sins. Not only will He fulfill our earnest prayers, but He makes intercession within us with groanings which cannot be uttered. Not only will He meet us in blessing if we will come to Him, but He will even take our will and work in us both to will and to do His good pleasure. His arms reach down to us at the lowest depth. His grace is beforehand in all its manifestations. Christ will take us at the very alphabet of Christian life and from the very beginning will count us His disciples and then will set us free. Let us fully learn this precious truth, and always take Him for the very thing we need the most and the first and even the very thing for which we ourselves are responsible and yet insufficient. He will not only do His glorious part, but He will enable us to do ours.

Relation to our Christian life and work

7. This expresses the relation of Christ to our Christian life and work. This is the true aim of a consecrated life—to make Jesus first. Let us give Him the first place in our heart, in our thoughts, in our aims and motives, in our plans, in our affections, friendships, occupations, our business, our pleasures, our families and our whole existence. Let us always come to Him first for help. Let us bring to Him the very first beginnings of temptation. Let us catch the lions and the dragons while they are young, and so shall we trample them under foot. And we will never see any old lions if

we do so without fail, for they will all be disposed of before they have time to grow formidable. Let us take to Him the merest thing that needs help, whether it be for soul or body, for secular business or sacred experiences. Jesus first—let this ever be our simple watchword, and life's tangles will all be unraveled, will not have time to grow serious, and so the touchstone that will settle every question of perplexity and duty will be Jesus first. Will I do this? Will I please this person or Him? Will it be something else, or will it be Jesus first? Oh, how this will consecrate, elevate and glorify our life and enthrone Him and us with Him in a kingdom of constant peace and victory! We must bring the crowns and lay them at His feet and write on everything: "From now on, Jesus first."

The Last

The eternal existence of Jesus

1. This implies the eternal existence of Jesus. He is, as He Himself expressed it, alive for evermore; or, as the old prophet put it still more sublimely, the Father of Eternity. It is glorious to have one that covers all the future and has in His hand the scroll of every destiny and the control of every future event. The Lamb in the midst of the throne holds the sealed book of all our destinies, and forevermore can fix every event of our existence. No matter what is coming, Jesus is coming with it. Though it be trial, temptation or death, He will be there. The heavens and the earth will pass away,

but He will remain. The friends we have known will disappear, but He will abide. We will change, but He is the same yesterday, today and forever. The things we commit to Him are committed against that day. The interests that He is guarding are safe forever. Beyond the smiling and the weeping, beyond the parting and the meeting, He stands in eternity with our title and our crown safe in His keeping. How often have we felt that the present sorrow or even death were nothing if it were all safe beyond, if it would be safe at last! Blessed be His name! He is the last, and His mighty works reach beyond all present vicissitudes and guard our treasures and trusts forevermore. The things He gives us will stand. The things that are linked with Him are eternal.

> There is One amid all changes
>   Who standeth ever fast;
> One who covers all the future,
>   The present and the past;
> Jesus is the Rock of Ages,
>   The first and the last.
> Jesus is the first;
>   Jesus is the last;
> Trust to Him thy future,
>   Give Him all thy past;
> Jesus is the Rock of Ages,
>   The first and the last.

Finish His work

2. Christ will finish His work in us and carry to

consummation all that He begins. Therefore, He is called "the author and perfecter of our faith" (Hebrews 12:2b). "He who began a good work in you will carry it on to completion until the day of Christ Jesus" (Philippians 1:6). "The Lord will fulfill his purpose for me" (Psalm 138:8a). "My sheep listen to my voice," He says, "and they shall never perish, no one can snatch them out of my hand" (John 10:27, 29). He takes us forever, and He will not leave us until He has done all that He has spoken of to us. He never leads His flock out to desert them in the hour of need. He never leads us out into the difficult enterprise without promising to stand by us and crown our work with success. He says of every true enterprise begun in His name and at His bidding, "The hands of Zerubbabel have laid the foundation of this temple; his hands will also complete it. Then you will know that the Lord Almighty has sent me to you" (Zechariah 4:9).

The end and substance

3. Christ is not only the finisher of our life and work, but Christ Himself is the end and substance of all things. When we are done with things and people and see Him as He is, we shall find that His heart is the fountain of all love, His smile the substance of all joy, His life the life of all life, Himself the first and the last of everything, and we will have nothing that is not part of Him and linked with Him. Every face we see will simply reflect His beauty. Every joy we feel will be but a radiant from His heart. Every glory we wear will be but a reflec-

tion of His holiness. Every throb of our immortal life will be but a pulsation of His being, and Christ shall be all, and in all, and we will have reached the last line of the old chorus, "Everything in Jesus, and Jesus in everything." So let us step out writing over every day and hour and moment, "Jesus first," and we will find surely that Jesus is "the last."

Christ the Living Way

Therefore, brothers, since we have confidence to enter the Most Holy Place by the blood of Jesus, by a new and living way opened for us through the curtain, that is, his body, and since we have a great priest over the house of God, let us draw near to God with a sincere heart in full assurance of faith, having our hearts sprinkled to cleanse us from a guilty conscience and having our bodies washed with pure water. Let us hold unswervingly to the hope we profess, for he who promised is faithful. And let us consider how we may spur one another on toward love and good deeds. (Hebrews 10:19–24)

These profound words tell us of five things: two things which we have, and three things which we are to do.

1. We have boldness to enter into the holiest by

the blood of Jesus. We see before us a model of the
ancient tabernacle—God's most perfect type of
Christ and our Christian life.

Entering the gate and the court, we ate beside
the altar of sacrifice and the laver of cleansing,
which tell us of Christ's atonement for our sins
and the Holy Spirit's cleansing work in our hearts.
Passing still further in through the door we come
to the Holy Place. The candlestick, the table of
shewbread and the altar of incense proclaim to us,
in symbol, the illumination of the Holy Spirit in
the heart where He dwells, the living bread with
which Jesus nourishes those who abide in Him, the
sweet communion with God, which that altar and
its incense set forth, and all that is meant by abiding in the secret place of the Most High and dwelling in intimate fellowship with Jesus.

Still further in stands the Holy of Holies,
separated only by the veil, and entered only by the
High Priest once a year on the Great Day of Atonement. It is the symbol of the presence and glory of
God, of the heavenly world and of the access into
it, which even here we may enjoy in the sweet fellowship of Jesus.

All this imagery is called up by the text. Dean Al-
ford translates the phrase, "Holy Place," and so
makes it mean all the chambers of the tabernacle,
even the court, and including the Holy of Holies.
Thus it would express all the fullness of our
spiritual privileges in Christ—the life in heavenly
places in Christ Jesus, as the apostle calls it in the
epistle to the Ephesians. Specially, however, it

refers to the inner chamber and expresses our complete and unobstructed access to all the fullness of God.

Had you stood in that tabernacle 3,000 years ago, you would have seen the view of that inner chamber obscured by the heavy veil covered with its symbolical embroideries which hung between. This veil and its embroideries spoke of Judaism and its types, which as yet obstructed the full view of the heavenly world and yet in a measure foreshadowed them. Had you stood in that tabernacle, however, on the Great Day of Atonement, you would have seen a solitary man, robed in priestly garments, pass through that veil with a censer full of burning coals and a bunch of hyssop saturated with sacrificial blood. For a moment he would stand within that holiest place and sprinkle that altar with the blood while he made intercession for the waiting congregation outside; and then you would have seen him retire with solemn awe, close the veil behind him and enter no more until the year was ended.

All this received its literal fulfillment on that day when, outside the eastern gate of Jerusalem, the Son of God died on Calvary, and His mortal flesh was rent by the death-stroke. Suddenly, the watchers in the temple beheld that mighty veil, that hung so high that human hands could not have reached it, rent asunder from top to bottom, proclaiming that henceforth the way to the holiest of all was opened, and that there was no barrier between the believing sinner and the holy God.

The way is opened

The way is opened to us to the altar of atonement for full and complete forgiveness, to the laver of cleansing for the washing of regeneration and the renewing of the Holy Ghost, to the golden candlestick for the fullness of the Holy Spirit's light and teaching, to the table of shewbread for the living bread which will sustain us in our spiritual and physical being, to the altar of incense for Christ's own intercession for us and constant access ourselves for communion with God.

The ark of the covenant, guarding and keeping for us God's holy law, tells us of our access to complete sanctification in Christ and the blood of sprinkling that keeps us ever accepted in His sight. We may come even to the very Shekinah of His presence to walk ever in the light of His countenance and dwell in the bosom of His love. Not timidly and with a sense of unworthiness are we to walk, but boldly, knowing that we are unworthy, but that Jesus Christ has purchased for us all these redemption rights and that we may fully claim them without doubt or fear. We have boldness by the blood of Jesus. We can take as much as that is worth. We were unworthy, but all has been covered by His satisfaction. We could not have come ourselves, but He has become our living way. We could not have put that veil aside, but God rent it from top to bottom through the death of His dear Son, and our crucifixion with Him, for the veil is His flesh.

In His earthly body He represented our sinful humanity, bore in His own person all the liabilities of lost men and was really counted a sinner in the eye of the law of God. That flesh stood between us and God; therefore it had to die in place of the guilty race, and when Christ's flesh was crucified on Calvary, it was the same as if the guilty race had been judged and slain. The obstruction was immediately removed and the way for access into the presence of God was opened.

There is a very deep spiritual application in all this for us. Before the Holy of Holies can be fully opened to our hearts and we can enter into the immediate presence and communion of God, the veil upon our hearts must be rent asunder, and this comes as it came on Calvary—by the death of our flesh. It is when we yield our own natural self to God to die and He slays us by the power of His Spirit that the obstruction to our communion with God is removed and we enter into its deeper fullness. The greatest hindrance to our peace and victory is the flesh. Whenever the consciousness of self rises vividly before you, and you become absorbed in your own troubles, cares, rights or wrongs, you at once lose communion with God, and a cloud of darkness falls over your spirit.

There is really nothing else that hurts or hinders us but this heavy weight of evil, this seed of Satan, this embodiment of the inmost essence of sin, this great mimic and antagonism of God, whose place it usurps, whose throne it claims, whose prerogatives it dares to monopolize. We can never rend it

asunder, but the Holy Spirit can. It dies only on
the cross of Jesus and on the pierced bosom of His
love, under the fire of His descending Spirit. Bring
it to Him, give Him the right to slay it, reckon it
dead, and then the veil will be rent asunder. The
Holy of Holies will open wide, the light of the
Shekinah will shine through all the house of God,
and the glory of heaven will be revealed in your
heart and life. Your inmost being will become like
that ancient tabernacle when illuminated by the
golden candlestick and the Shekinah of God's
visible presence.

2. We have a High Priest over the house of God.
Not only have we a home to shelter us, but we have
an Elder Brother to welcome and love us.

The ministry of the ancient high priest was very
important. It was he that opened the way into the
holiest and made reconciliation for the sins of the
people. So our great High Priest has opened for us
the way and keeps it ever open, "because he always
lives to intercede for [us]" (Hebrews 7:25b). It is
His business to settle for us the question of our
sins and to keep us cleansed from their power and
saved from their effects.

The time to go to Him is not when you feel
strong in your victories, but when baffled, defeated
and crushed by temptation and conscious unworthiness. He that washed the disciples' feet still
stands in the heavenly court girded with the towel
of priestly service and with open bosom ready to
pour His precious blood over all your stains. Let
us, therefore, come boldly to the throne of grace

even to obtain mercy, as well as to find grace to help in time of need.

The ancient priest also ministered to the suffering and the sick. It was his business to inspect the leper, to offer the sacrifices for his cleansing, to pronounce him clean. And so our great High Priest is also our great Physician and heals all our diseases, comforts all our sorrows and binds up our broken hearts. He is able to be touched with feelings of our infirmities, for He was "tempted in every way, just as we are—yet was without sin" (Hebrews 4:15b).

Also, he bore upon his shoulders and upon his breast in jeweled letters the names of Israel's tribes, and so Christ bears us upon the shoulders of His strength and the bosom of His love in unceasing faithfulness and unfailing strength. He presents our prayers before the throne with acceptance to His Father and ours. He keeps our relations with God always right. He remembers us in constant intercession, even when we ourselves may not know our need, nor what to pray for as we ought.

In a word, He superintends and carries on the entire business of our spiritual life and is for us "the author and perfecter of our faith." We have such a High Priest. He is there in our behalf. He has been appointed by His Father for this great business. He has accepted Him as such; He belongs to us. Let us make use of this glorious opportunity, and "since we have a great high priest who has gone through the heavens, Jesus the Son of God, let us hold firmly to the faith we profess. . . . Let us then approach the throne of grace with confidence, so that we may receive mercy and find grace to help us in our time of need" (Hebrews 4:14–16).

What we should do

1. "Let us draw near." This is to say, let us not live a distant, cold and timid life, but let us enter into all the fullness of our privileges and live in the intimate friendship of our Savior. Let us come with a single purpose to please and obey Him with a true heart and an honest single aim. Let us come in full assurance of faith, not timidly dreading a reproof or a blow, but sweetly knowing that we are welcome and like a happy child pressing right into the bosom of our Father. And even if we are conscious of unworthiness, let us come with a heart sprinkled from an evil conscience and bodies washed with pure water. There is cleansing for us, if we have erred, in that precious blood and that renewing Spirit's grace, and not even our imperfections should keep us back from communion with God and the joy of His presence.

It is a very beautiful provision of the old time that the blemished priest might not minister at the altar, but he may eat of the priestly bread. A broken limb or a crooked joint disqualified him from standing at the altar as an officiating priest but not from entering the Holy place and feeding upon the provisions for the priesthood. This is a beautiful token that Christ's most imperfect children are welcome to His love and grace and may ever draw near for His help and comfort, and while this must not encourage weakness, yet let it ever keep us from discouragements and constrain us to draw still nearer to His breast and so to live that we shall ever please Him, and not have sin to bring Him, but grateful love and holy service.

Hold fast unswervingly

2. "Let us hold unswervingly to the hope we profess, for he who promised is faithful" (Hebrews 10:23). This hope of ours and this faith refer to the great eternal goal of faith and hope—our complete salvation through Christ Jesus. But it also applies to every confidence which God has given to us and every promise which He has permitted us to claim.

Let us stand steadfastly in the trust which He has given us, and let us do so without a faltering movement or a trembling fiber. Let us stand unshaken in our confidence, and let us do so because He stands firmly at the other end. The cable yonder is fastened round the throne. Let it be fastened around our hearts in inflexible and immovable security and thus standing upon His promises and holding fast our confidence, He is not hindered on His side in fulfilling all His purposes of blessing.

Spur one another on

3. "Let us consider how we may spur one another on toward love and good deeds" (Hebrews 10:24). Such glorious privileges should make us unselfish and devoted and find expression in lives of loving service. As travelers ascending dangerous

mountains tie their bodies together with strong cords, so that if one should fall the others will support him, so God has linked our hearts and lives together by innumerable cords of sympathy, suffering and mutual influence. If one member suffers, all suffer.

We who have entered into the holiest and are walking into the inner presence of God particularly are expected to be loving, cheerful and helpful to one another and to bear the burdens of the weak and suffering. The best evidence you can give that you are a strong Christian is to bear the infirmities of the weak and not to please yourself. "For even Christ did not please himself but, as it is written; 'The insults of those who insult you have fallen on me' " (Romans 15:3). Therefore let us consider one another, hold up each other, bear one another's burdens and so fulfill the law of Christ. Let us carry one another in the sweet ministry of prayer. Let us be patient with each other. Let us be very considerate of each other's faults and failings, and let us prove that we have indeed a deeper life and a fuller blessing by pouring it out abundantly on those who lack.

Such, then, beloved, are our privileges and responsibilities. Let us more fully possess the former, and more faithfully will we perform the latter. More intimately let us draw near, more constantly let us dwell in the secret of His presence, and more faithfully will we fulfill our duties to others in every earthly relationship, and let us do this so much the more as we see the day approaching. Our Lord is coming before long, and this blessed hope, if fully realized, will make all our trials, irritations and provocations seem light and small in comparison with the one great object of winning His approval and wearing the crown which He will give to all who overcome.

Christ Our Surety

But the ministry Jesus has received is as superior to theirs as the covenant of which he is mediator is superior to the old one, and it is founded on better promises. (Hebrews 8:6)

For no matter how many promises God has made, they are "Yes" in Christ. And so through him the "Amen" is spoken by us to the glory of God. (2 Corinthians 1:20)

Is not my house right with God?/ Has he not made with me an everlasting covenant,/ arranged and secured in every part?/ Will he not bring to fruition my salvation and grant me my every desire? (2 Samuel 23:5).

Covenants are more common and more sacred in Oriental countries than in western society.

The Arab chief will guard with his life the person with whom he has made the covenant of bread and salt. God has accommodated Himself to human speech and customs by revealing the glorious plan of mercy to us under the figure of a covenant, and has bound Himself to us by bonds so secure and sacred that they are an anchor of the soul, both sure and steadfast, if we have fled for refuge to the hope set before us in the gospel.

The covenant of redemption

This takes us away back to the ages before the fall and the revelation of God's mercy. In the counsels of eternity the covenant was made between the Father and the Son. Then it was that, foreseeing the ruin that was to come upon the human race through the awful power of sin, God the Father entered into a covenant with His beloved Son, guaranteeing to Him, on condition that He should assume the liabilities and the nature of the fallen race, to give to Him for them a complete salvation.

On the part of Christ it was necessary that He should take the sinner's place; that He should stoop from His high and exalted position and become not only a man, but a despised and rejected man, a man of sorrows; that He should bear the taunts and cruelties of man, the pains of death, the assaults and insults of the devil and all his regions of the dead and the throne of intercession as a merciful High Priest, bearing the burdens of His people, making continual intercession for them, enduring their provocations, infirmities and failures and guarding them with unceasing love, until His work might be completed in all their lives.

On the Father's part, He promised on account of the fulfillment of these conditions that He should give eternal life to all that received His Son and freely forgive and justify them from all their transgressions and create within them a new heart. He also promised that His Holy Spirit should sanctify and perfect them in holiness, should supply to them all needed grace, power, love and blessing, should accept them as the sons of God, make them the heirs of His glory and partakers of the divine nature, and should at last raise them from the dead and glorify them with Jesus in the ages to come, with a place of honor and blessing higher than Adam ever knew, higher than angels will ever possess, and more than compensating for all the evils and miseries of the fall.

This covenant Jesus Christ accepted. "Here I am, I have come!" was His glad answer, "to do your will, O my God;/ your law is within my heart" (Psalm 40:7a, 8). And so He came, lived, loved and died, and at last could say, in His closing prayer, as He committed His work to the Father, "I have brought you glory on earth by completing the work you gave me to do" (John 17:4), and on the cross could shout, "It is finished" (John 19:30).

Then the Father put His seal upon the finished work by raising Him from the dead, and so declaring forever that the covenant had been fulfilled, the conditions met and the great redemption com-

pleted. Christ's ascension from the tomb was the
seal of this; the coming of the Holy Ghost on the
day of Pentecost was a second seal; the conversion
of every believer since had been a further seal that
the covenant is ratified and forever holds fast.
Every answer to prayer in the name of Jesus, every
blessing that comes to our spiritual life, is an echo
from the cross repeating, "It is finished"; and we
know that the covenant is fulfilled, and "arranged
and secured in every part" (2 Samuel 23:5b). This
is the ground of our salvation. It is not because we
have a covenant with God, but Jesus has; and we
simply accept Him. We come into His covenant, for
He could say to the Father, "You granted him
authority over all people that he might give eternal
life to all those you have given him" (John 17:2);
and then He could add, "protect them by the power
of your name—the name you gave me—so that
they may be one as we are one" (John 17:11b).

Our salvation, therefore, is wholly dependent
upon our accepting Jesus, and this brings to us all
the promises of the covenant that He has ratified
and fulfilled. Therefore, "no matter how many
promises God has made, they are 'Yes,' in Christ"
(2 Corinthians 1:20a). Therefore, to the last moment of our life, we have no personal claim upon
God for anything. Everything we receive is the infinite mercy of God in Christ and for His sake; and
to the last breath of life, we will never receive anything that is not the pure undeserved mercy of God
for His sake. How very simple this makes salvation!
How very strong our consummation in Christ!

How very sacred our hope! How mighty the anchor that holds us in the storm of temptation and doubt and fear!

The revelation of God's covenant

The law of Moses was not the covenant of God which He designed to be His permanent bond of union with His people. It was simply a temporary revelation, similar to the covenant of works made at the creation of man, which God knew they would not keep, and which was designed, not to save men, not to sanctify them, but to reveal to them their sin and to show the need of a higher covenant of grace and mercy in Christ, even the covenant of grace which Christ has brought in.

The first full revelation of God's covenant of grace was made to Abraham, and the covenant of Abraham still holds good for all believers. This was not intended for the Jewish people exclusively, but was designed to include all the children of faith, of whom Abraham was the spiritual father. This the apostle clearly teaches us in the epistle to the Galatians, where he tells us that "those who believe are children of Abraham. The Scripture foresaw that God would justify the Gentiles by faith, and announced the gospel in advance to Abraham: 'All nations will be blessed through you.' So those who have faith are blessed along with Abraham, the man of faith" (3:7–9).

The essence of the covenant with Abraham was the promise of the seed, and this was Christ, so that Abraham's covenant was just that Jesus was to come and do all things in accordance with the eternal covenant of redemption, of which we have previously spoken.

This covenant Abraham received in the simplest way by naked faith, but he did not do anything to deserve it. He just believed God. God came to him with a revelation of His promise and mercy, and Abraham accepted it like a child and began to act accordingly, and his life was simply one of trust and trustful obedience. For this, God blessed him with His friendship and made him father of all who have since been received into that covenant friendship.

Much more fully in the later Scriptures do we find this covenant unfolding. Particularly in the writings of Jeremiah does God reveal to His people, in the darkest hour of their sin and suffering, His future plans of grace and mercy. "The time is coming," we read in Jeremiah 31:31–34:

> "when I will make a new covenant
>   with the house of Israel
>   and with the house of Judah.
> It will not be like the covenant
>   I made with their forefathers
> when I took them by the hand
>   to lead them out of Egypt,
> because they broke my covenant,
>   though I was a husband to them,"
>   declares the LORD.
> "This is the covenant I will make with the
>   house of Israel

after that time," declares the LORD.
"I will put my law in their minds
    and write it on their hearts.
I will be their God,
    and they will be my people.
No longer will a man teach his neighbor,
or a man his brother, saying, 'Know the
        LORD,'
because they will all know me,
    from the least of them to the greatest,"
        declares the LORD.
"For I will forgive their wickedness,
    and will remember their sins no more."

That this is the covenant of the gospel is perfectly certain from the fact that in the epistle to the
Hebrews it is twice quoted by the Holy Ghost as
the rule of God's dealings with His people today
and as the bond into which He brings them in
Jesus Christ, who is the surety of this better
covenant established upon better promises.

Promises of the covenant

The promises of this covenant are very wonderful. The first of them is our sanctification. It is very
glorious that the thing that God first undertakes to
do is to make and keep us right. Instead of giving
us an outward law and compelling us to keep it
without power, He promises to put it in our hearts,
to make us live it, to make us incorporate it into
our being, to enshrine it in our affections, to make

it our very nature, until we shall live it and keep it, spontaneously, joyfully, lovingly and with our whole heart. This is what the Holy Spirit does, and therefore, on the day of Pentecost, the anniversary of the giving of law, He came to be the inner law of holiness and power in every believer's heart.

Next, He promises to be our God. He next comes to us to be our all-sufficiency for every need. He lets us own Him and possess Him as our God and use Him in His infinite resources for every need. Further, He promises that we will know the Lord for ourselves and have His light and guidance, not being dependent upon others to teach, but receiving directly from His will and mind for us.

Finally, it includes complete forgiveness and eternal obliteration of all sin and transgression, the blotting out of the past, entire justification, and the treating of His children as if they had not sinned.

Beloved, will you take this mighty covenant? It is yours by purchase of the Redeemer's blood; and if you simply accept Jesus, "how will he not also, along with him, graciously give us all things" (Romans 8:32b)? What can you need besides this mighty provision?

The security of this covenant

He says, "[It is] an everlasting covenant,/ arranged and secured in every part" (2 Samuel 23:5). Again He says, " 'Though the mountains be shaken and the hills be removed,/ yet my unfailing love for you will not be shaken/ nor my covenant of peace be removed,' says the Lord, who has compassion on you" (Isaiah 54:10).

The reason it is so secure is that it is not dependent upon us at all, but on its great surety, the Lord Jesus Christ. If we were dependent upon our works in the slightest particular, we should fail and wreck all our prospects. But He has confirmed it and therefore it must stand, and if we simply stand in Him, trusting and following Him, He will accomplish all its provisions in us and for us. Therefore the apostle says, "Therefore, the promise comes by faith, that it may be by grace and may be guaranteed to all Abraham's offspring" (Romans 4:16a). If it had been of works it could not have been sure; but it is by faith, and faith in nothing but receiving a gift, thanking Him for it, and continuing to trust Him for it.

Again, it is sure because God not only promised it, but He has covenanted it and sworn to it. The very strongest language has been employed to emphasize the absolute security of this great promise of mercy, "that, by two unchangeable things in which it is impossible for God to lie, we who have fled to take hold of the hope offered to us may be greatly encouraged" (Hebrews 6:18). If we simply have fled for refuge and are holding fast to our hope in Christ and to Christ our hope, the anchor must hold amid all the storms of doubt and temptation.

Again, it is secure because it is based on God's pure mercy and not upon our deserving. He takes us from the beginning and He holds us to the end as the children of His mercy. It is not merely that He takes us at first in mercy and afterwards treats us according to our deserving, but all the way along we must recognize ourselves as worthless and undeserving, living upon His mercy, and saved and sanctified through His free grace.

Therefore our very sanctification, instead of being a merit, is simply a richer mercy, and the apostle says, "those who receive God's abundant provision of grace and of the gift of righteousness reign in life through the one man, Jesus Christ" (Romans 5:17b).

It is so sweet to feel that we are ever lying in the bosom of His mercy, and that we claim His great salvation with the consciousness of our nothingness and worthlessness and yet of our infinite and everlasting life in Christ! Therefore the apostle has said that "no matter how many promises God has made, they are 'Yes' in Christ" (2 Corinthians 1:20a). Everything we ever claim in answer to believing prayer must come through His mercy and covenant; but we claim that all for this great reason, "for Jesus' sake." They all are yes at the beginning, and shall be amen at the end, for we simply claim them and hold to them for His sake and in His name. He is the surety of our covenant.

His secure and everlasting covenant

Or, will we say that the yes is God's assurance, His repeated word, His second immutable thing, and the Amen is the echo of our faith as it takes Him at His word and declares it shall be done.

Thank God for His secure and everlasting covenant. Thank God that in Christ it covers us. Let us take it, and let our names be written in it afresh and cover with it all our future way.

Let us cover with it our sins behind, our hearts within, our way before, our hours of temptation and conflict, our hours of service, our ignorance and helplessness, our perils and our paths of difficulty all the way down to the tomb, all the way up to His coming. It covers all right up to the throne; and the anchor will hold, until, within the veil, all the storms are past and the surges swell no more, and we will say around the throne, with a great shout, "Salvation belongs to our God,/ who sits on the throne,/ and to the Lamb" (Revelation 7:10).

Have you been thinking mostly of your faith and your works and your fidelity to God? Have you not, perhaps been somewhat under the covenant of Sinai, and therefore weakened and crushed? Oh! hasten to Calvary, and take refuge in the hope set before you in the gospel with a heart humbly and simply yielded to Jesus. Take His great covenant rather than yours, and rest in His faithful and everlasting pledge to carry you through all. Say, "Who shall separate us from the love of Christ" (Romans 8:35a)? It is not the babe's arms that hold the mother; but the mother's arms that hold the babe.

> It's not my love to Thee,
>   That I delight to tell,
> But on Thy love, O Christ to me,
>   How I delight to dwell!

Ere the curtain rose,
　Or angels sang above,
The records of the past disclose,
　Thine everlasting love.

Lord, help me to believe
　Thy wondrous love to me,
So shall my heart more fully give,
　Thine own love back to Thee.

Christ Our Passover

*Get rid of the old yeast [leaven, KJV]
that you may be a new batch without
yeast—as you really are. For Christ, our
Passover lamb, has been sacrificed.
Therefore let us keep the Festival, not
with the old yeast, the yeast of malice
and wickedness, but with bread without
yeast, the bread of sincerity and truth. (1
Corinthians 5:7–8)*

The Jewish Passover is one of the most lasting
memorials of God's covenant with His ancient people. After 3,000 years have passed away,
after temple and tabernacle worship have ceased,
after the scattering of Israel's sons in another land,
after the cessation of sacrifices and ceremonial
worship in almost every other particular, after the
treading down of Jerusalem for nearly 12 centuries, you can still find as every Nisan returns
every Hebrew household in the world gathering
around their table at the evening hour of the Pas-

sover week. They eat the flesh of the lamb and the
unleavened cakes with bitter herbs, and the father
of the household, with lighted candle, passes
through the chambers and searches under every
article of furniture to see if he can find a single
particle of leaven, and then solemnly pronounces
that all the leaven is cast out. They sit down
together under the sprinkled blood and partake of
the paschal supper. How vividly it all interprets the
words of our text, "Christ, our Passover lamb has
been sacrificed. Therefore let us keep the Festival,
not with the old yeast, the yeast of malice and
wickedness, but with bread without yeast, the
bread of sincerity and truth."

The paschal lamb

In the book of Exodus we find the story of the
first Passover. It was the beginning of months to
Israel, even as the acceptance of Christ as our
Savior is to us the beginning of life's record in its
eternal form.

1. The first thing was the selecting of the lamb.
It was chosen on the 10th day of the month, the
time suggesting the fullness of the time when God
sent forth His Son. The lamb was first separated
and set apart for three and a half days under the
observation of all the people and known to be
without blemish and without spot. Even so at His
baptism on the banks of the Jordan, the Lord Jesus
Christ was set apart by the Holy Ghost for three
and a half years to the observation of all men
before He was sacrificed for the sins of the world.

2. The lamb was unblemished. So Christ was perfectly harmless, undefiled and separate from sinners, with no guilt of His own to expiate and therefore wholly free to be an atonement for the world. His perfection was witnessed by all men. His blamelessness could be seen in all possible circumstances. His life was as open as the noontide blaze, and none could find fault with Him in anything that He ever said or did. Even in the judgment of His enemies it was the most perfect and beautiful life ever lived below the skies. Even if there would have been no historical Christ, the Christ of the gospels is a faultless and irreproachable picture, which infidelity gazes upon with astonishment and admiration.

3. The lamb was next slain by the congregation of Israel. And so Christ was sacrificed by the decision of the Jewish Sanhedrin and the act of the entire nation and was thus in some sense the public and official oblation made by them for their sins. The words of Caiaphas just before his death has a peculiar significance, which he did not understand. "It is better," he said, "that one man die for the people than that the whole nation perish" (John 11:50). Thus Judaism, like the great High Priest, offered up its own Messiah as a sacrifice and an offering for the sins of the world; and as they gazed upon the heaving chest, the failing breath and the flowing blood of that gentle lamb, how vividly they must have realized the meaning of sin and the cost of salvation! Even so we still behold the dying agonies of the Lamb of God, and in the

memorial of His death realize afresh that "He was led like a lamb to the slaughter,/ and as a sheep before her shearers is silent,/ so he did not open his mouth" (Isaiah 53:7b).

> Mercy's streams in streams of blood,
> Plenteous grace our soul bedewing,
> Plead and claim our peace with God.

What was the full significance of that death? It was the substitute for their death. The first-born of Egypt fell before the destroyer's stroke, but the death took the place of their own death, and they escaped. And so, for our life His life is the sacrifice, and with that blood over us our spiritual life is redeemed and our physical life is safe until His will shall call it home. No destroying angel can touch us, though he may hover near, as long as we are under the blood and that death is our substitute and sacrifice.

4. The blood of the lamb was sprinkled upon the door posts and lintel of every home. It is not enough that Christ should be sacrificed; He must also be appropriated by each for himself. It is very sweet to know that the sprinkling was not done by other hands, but each household sprinkled its own door. So can each of us apply to ourselves the precious blood of our Redeemer. It was freely shed for all, and each of us can take it as freely as we may. How precious to know that this blood is for us still! Take it, and you can cover yourself from this very moment so that no angel of destruction can touch

your being. You will stand by the very throne of God sheltered from all harm in the precious blood of Christ. You have come " . . . to the sprinkled blood that speaks a better word than the blood of Abel" (Hebrews 12:24b). Have you applied it? Apply it now and ever walk under its sheltering, cleansing covering.

The feast

Not only was there a sacrifice, but there was also a feast. Not only was the blood shed for the remission of our sins, but the life of our dear Lord was also given us for our life. They were to eat the flesh of the lamb as well as sprinkle its blood. It is not even necessary to say that this represents Christ's own very life given to us as the food and nourishment of our whole being. "I am the living bread . . . If anyone eats of this bread, he will live forever. This bread is my flesh, which I will give for the life of the world. . . . For my flesh is real food and my blood is real drink" (John 6:51, 55). They were to eat the whole lamb, with the head, the legs and the purtenance thereof; and so we are to feed on the whole of Christ. We need His head for our thoughts. "We have the mind of Christ" (1 Corinthians 2:16b). We need His legs for our walk and the purtenance thereof covers everything that pertains to our life, and so there is nothing but Christ covers, supplies, fills. They were to leave none of it until the morning, and so there is nothing in Jesus that we can afford to leave unappropriated. He wants to fill all our life, to satisfy all our being and to lead each one of us into the very fullness of union with Him in every particular. Let us take our sacrificial feast. It is not merely food; it is a feast. God does not merely supply all our necessities; He gives us abundance, wine upon the lees, fatness full of marrow, overflowing and boundless grace and blessing. So let us keep this sacred feast.

They were not to eat of it raw, but cooked with fire; and so the Holy Ghost must prepare Christ for us and make Him to be suitable nourishment. He only can; and He loves to minister Jesus to the hungry and thirsty heart, to take His fullness and feed it into us, until every part of our being is sweetly satisfied and strengthened by the living bread. And they were to eat this feast together. It was not a solitary meal. It is not possible for you or me to take Christ alone in all His fullness.

It is with all saints that we enter into the height and depth and breadth of the love of Christ which transcends knowledge. The more narrow and isolated you are in your Christian life, the less full and rich it will be; and the larger your heart and the fuller your fellowship in Him, the more of Him will you enjoy.

If their family was not big enough, they were to take in the stranger; and so God wants some of us to enlarge our circle of love, to unite our hearts with others in the full fellowship of holy love, fitly framed together to grow up into all the maturity of our Christian life.

There were some bitter herbs in this feast, but they only added zest to the sacred meal, even as our trials are turned into blessings and become the bittersweet of life when truly sanctified by the Holy Ghost to a loving, obedient heart.

The leaven (yeast)

This represents the elements of corruption, fermentation, impurity. Therefore we are to purge out the old leaven that we may be a new batch, because we are unleavened. The leaven represents all that which is earthly and sinful, and we may know the leaven by its effects. That which produces the ferment of earthly passion, agitation and unrest, selfish and unholy desire, rebellion against God, disobedience and sin, is leaven. There are two leavens. There is the old leaven, the natural life which God wants us to lay down and be taken up in His pure and heavenly life. And then there is a worse leaven, the leaven of malice and wickedness. All this must be purged out.

The purging is sometimes severe, for the evil is obstinate. As we have already said, the Jewish father searches the house with lighted candle to see if there is crumb of leaven, and having done so, he solemnly pronounces the house to be clean. So with the Word of God, we are to pass through the chambers of our heart, and having found any evil thing, cast it out, lay it down at the feet of Christ and under the blood. And when we can find nothing for which our heart can condemn us, we are to rest, we are to pronounce the house clean, the lump unleavened and hear the Master say to our peaceful heart, "You are already clean because of the word I have spoken to you. Remain in me, and I will remain in you" (John 15:3–4a).

God does not want us to be in continual unrest and self-reproof, but in quietness and confidence to trust Him to keep us pure and holy. The enemy will love to sit upon us in judgment and to have us to help him, but this is not primitive of holiness any more than the opening up of the grave and the upturning of the bones of the dead could be primitive of health. Let us walk in innocency of heart, believing that we please God and sweetly resting in His love. We cannot purge out the old leaven, but we can give it to Christ, and He will cleanse us by His own precious blood and Holy Spirit. And having yielded up to Him, we must believe that He does cleanse us, and walk in simple faith and self-forgetfulness, with holy vigilance, and yet with holy confidence in His leading and keeping grace and power.

The bread

"The [unleavened] bread of sincerity and truth." Not only are we to be ourselves unleavened, but our daily bread must be unleavened. We cannot feed upon mixed food. The cause of weakness and suffering in most cases is that we feed so much upon earthly diet and forbidden bread. Sincerity literally means singleness, and truth suggests the idea of God's Word, which is indeed our daily food. As we feed upon it unmixed with the exciting thoughts of man, we will be fed and nourished in all godliness and sincerity, and we will grow in grace and in the knowledge of our Lord and Savior Jesus Christ.

The journey

They were to eat their Passover meal in haste, with loins girded and shoes on their feet and staves in their hands. They were to go on their way further to their full inheritance. And so we go forth from the Passover to all the fullness of our Father's will and our future inheritance. Let our loins be girded for service. Let our feet be shod for our holy race. Let our hands hold the hand of promise. Let our vision be set firmly toward His coming and all His holy will. Thus covered with His blood and feeding upon His flesh, separated from all evil and pressing on behind the pillar of cloud that leads our way, let us walk as strangers and pilgrims upon the earth, looking and hastening unto the coming of our Lord and preparing for it by lives of holy service and consecration.

Christ Our Prophet

*This is that Moses who told the Is-
raelites, "God will send you a prophet
like me from your own people." (Acts
7:37)*

The Hebrew prophets were the noblest class of
men in ancient Israel. The priests were not
always pure and true to God, for even the sons of
Aaron brought dishonor upon themselves in the
first generation; and the kings with few exceptions
were unfaithful and unholy in the influence of
their lives.

The very best of them, David, Jehoshaphat,
Hezekiah and Josiah, were marked by the strongest
imperfections, and many of them were blots upon
the history of their country. But the prophets of Israel were always true, from Moses, the first
glorious leader and teacher of God's inheritance, to
John the Baptist, who closed the ancient dispensation and ushered in the new. They were all types of
the great Prophet, whom Stephen announced as

their divine successor, and the great apostle and
prophet of our profession, Jesus Christ. Let us look
at His prophetic office as it is illustrated by their
function and their lives.

The functions of our Great Prophet

1. In general, the ancient prophet was the messenger of God to the people and the representative
of His will concerning them. So Jesus Christ to us
is the messenger of Jehovah, the Word of God, the
voice of divine authority and divine love, who
brings to us God's will and reveals to us His plan of
salvation and life.

2. More particularly He is our Teacher, leading
us into all truth and building us up in our faith
and life. It is He who gives us the first ray of light
that dawns upon the darkness of the natural heart.
It is He who shows to us ourselves and Himself and
enables us to trust Him as our Savior. It is He who
opens our inner eyes to see the light that streams
from heaven through the Word. It is He who shows
to us the deeper truths of the Christ life: Himself
as our Sanctifier, our Life, our Healer, our help in
every time of need. It is He who, as fast as we
believe, enlarges our vision, our hope, our desire,
our knowledge, our faith and shows us the King in
His beauty and the land that is afar off. It is He
who anoints our eyes with salve that we may see
and then opens to us the light which we are able to
receive. It is He who makes the truth not only light
but life and enables us to appropriate it, to believe
it, to feed upon it, to be strengthened, quickened

and sanctified by it. He is our wonderful Counselor, our unerring Teacher, our faithful Prophet.

3. As our Prophet He guides us in perplexity and shows us the way we should go. He not only gives us truths, but light upon our path. "Whoever follows me will never walk in darkness, but will have the light of life" (John 8:12b). The ancient prophets were the counselors of the king and the nations in hours of perplexity. Nathan came to David with the Lord's word concerning his important acts. Elisha was the counselor of the king. Samuel was the guide of Israel. Jesus is our leader and guide. When He puts us forth, He goes before us and the sheep follow Him, for they know His voice. He will not let us err. He will lead us in a straight way, wherein we will not stumble, and He will stay with us nearest of all in the dark perplexities and crises of life.

4. As our Prophet He unfolds the vision of the future, showing us His plan concerning the world and the church, especially His own personal coming, preparing us to work for Him in intelligent hope and cooperation, and showing us as much of His plan for His own life as we need to know to inspire us with courage and enable us to meet with intelligence the duties and claims of life. He whispers to our hearts the assurance of His answer to our prayers, leads out our new hopes in holy aspirations for service and blessing and gives us glimpses of the great and mighty things He would have us aspire to and expect from Him.

5. As our Prophet He is the great wonder

Worker, for the prophets of old not only brought the message of God, but accredited it by signs and wonders, proving by their supernatural working that their message was indeed divine. So our Lord Jesus Christ, our own dear Prophet, brings us not only words, but deeds, fulfills what He commands and ever seals His message to us by His own omnipotent and blessed working.

Illustrations of Christ's prophetic work

Moses

1. In Moses we behold the first type of our great Prophet. Born of the oppressed race, he was one of them and could come near to their hearts in deepest sympathy. So Christ is a brother born of our flesh and blood, and further, a brother born for adversity. He was the revealer of God's purpose of deliverance and redemption to them, and he led them out of Egypt into their covenant with Jehovah. So Christ reveals to us the great redemption and leads us into it. He was the revealer to them of the law of God and the gospel, as unfolded in the wondrous tabernacle and types; and so Jesus Christ is our Teacher, not only of moral and spiritual truth, but especially of salvation, that glorious salvation of which the ancient tabernacle was the wondrous type.

Above all else, he was their devoted, faithful and unwavering friend, utterly true to their interests amid the great discouragement and provocation, and never failing them even when they failed him and proved wholly unfaithful to their God. How often they disappointed him and provoked their God, but never once did he falter in his faithful love. How often did they speak against Moses and Jehovah, murmuring in the wilderness, but he ever met them with new light and deliverance. And even when Jehovah seemed for a moment about to reject them and offered Moses a new inheritance of his own if he would give them up, Moses refused and offered himself a sacrifice for the people he loved, crying, "But now, please forgive their sin—but if not, then blot me out of the book you have written" (Exodus 32:32).

Again, when a more terrible crisis came and they refused to enter the land of promise and were driven back into the wilderness for 40 years to perish in their unbelief, Moses did not leave them but went back with them every step of the way, clinging to his unworthy children with more than a mother's love until once more he brought them to the borders of their inheritance which he lost through their provocation.

What a beautiful type of the more gracious, tender, faithful Prophet whom we follow! How often we grieve Him, and how faithfully He loves us and keeps us, "because God has said, 'Never will I leave you;/ never will I forsake you' " (Hebrews 13:5b), until He will have accomplished all His gracious will for all of us! More than the love of Moses is the love of Jesus! How we have proved that love already! We can trust it still, for He has said, " 'Though the mountains be shaken/ and the hills be removed/ yet my unfailing love for you will not be shaken/ nor my covenant of peace be removed,'/ says the Lord, who has compassion on you" (Isaiah 54:10).

Samuel

2. Samuel, the great reformer, was the prophet of Israel's return to God from the dark and long apostasy under the judges, when for 400 years the light of God's covenant presence was almost extinguished. He was the prophet who established the whole school of Hebrew prophets, and so shaped and formed out of the chaos of sin and wretchedness amid which he was born, the elements of unity, strength and stability in the kingdom of David, which he left as his heritage to Israel, and which were far more the work of his life than even of David's own faith and fidelity to God. Samuel, the faithful friend of weak and inconsistent Israel, expressed his noble spirit in the words which he said to them on one occasion, "Far be it from me that I should sin against the Lord by failing to pray for you. And I will teach you the way that is good and right" (1 Samuel 12:23). Samuel was the type of Jesus, the prophet of the poor backslider, the Christ that restored Peter and Thomas, and still tenderly and faithfully awaits to welcome back the wanderer to His bosom again. How tenderly He loves the contrite heart! How graciously He restores the child! How sweetly He forgives! How mightily He keeps! How faithfully He loves! How perfectly He heals our backsliding and becomes the

dew upon Israel, revives us as the corn, causes us to grow as the vine and our scent as Lebanon. He leads us on and up until we are established, strengthened, built up and settled, and become like Israel of old, His own royal kingdom and throne.

Elijah

3. Elijah tells us of the great prophet of reproof and correction, the loving teacher who has sometimes to show us our faults and to chasten us for them in tender love. Elijah was the faithful reprover of sin and represented the judicial element in God. So our great Prophet has often to correct His people and show them their faults and lead them from the error of their ways by His heart-searching discipline. But He is a better reprover than Elijah; for there is no better evidence than the life of Elijah himself of the failure of even that greatest of prophets and the tender faithfulness of the true Prophet who dealt with him as He does with us. Would we see the true spirit of Jesus our Prophet?

Let us look at the God of Elijah, as the poor broken prophet lies under the juniper tree, a fugitive and a failure after the highest triumph of his glorious life. How gently God deals with him! He first rests him with sleep and then feeds him by angel hands, then sends him alone to Horeb and asks him, "What are you doing here, Elijah" (1 Kings 19:9b)? True, He speaks with the earthquake, the whirlwind and the fire, but He ends with the still, small voice. The last message is

a restoration of his commission and a renewal of
his call to service as He sends him forth to anoint
Jehu, Hazael and Elisha for the work that yet
remains to be done. So gently yet faithfully does
our dear Prophet teach us; not crushing the spirit
that would fail before Him or the souls that He has
made, but tenderly leading us into all His light and
then making the very best of us, notwithstanding
our worst failures. Let us never doubt our faithful
Christ, our wonderful Counselor, our mighty God,
our everlasting Father, our Prince of Peace.

Elisha

4. The most beautiful prophetic life of the Old
Testament was that of Elisha, and he is a perfect
type of Jesus Christ, our Prophet. Elijah represented the law; Elisha, the gospel. Elijah, the discipline of judgment; Elisha, the salvation of grace.
Elijah was the thunderbolt and lightning; Elisha,
the sunshine and light. Elijah was the woodman's
axe and fire; Elisha, the husbandman with his seed
and watering pot, with fields of green and harvests
of golden grain. Elisha's is the ministry of love—
the ministry of Jesus. He begins by healing the bar-
ren land and the water by sprinkling salt in its
fountains. He was like the great Prophet who does
not blame the outflowing of our lives so much, but
rather goes to the fountainhead and heals the
source of our thoughts, motives and actions by the
touch of His mighty love.

Look at him again as he meets the baffled kings
of Judah, Israel and Edom in the valley of death

and famine. Instead of blaming them for their mistake, he gently interposes for their deliverance, commands the valley to be filled with ditches, claims from heaven the floods of water to fill all the mighty spaces and overflow in blessing for the perishing armies.

So our great Prophet comes to us in the calamities that we have brought upon ourselves, and delivers us, and then gently leads us to greater blessings.

Look at him again as the poor widow appeals to him for help against the creditors who are about to seize upon her sons for her debts. "What do you have in your house?" (2 Kings 4:2) is all he asks. Then he commands the pot of oil to be brought forth and poured into all the empty vessels she can find or borrow until they are filled to overflowing, and she is rich with a harvest of faith. Finally he bids her sell the oil, pay her debts and live upon the rest.

So our great Prophet meets us in every emergency by showing us that we have within our house the one remedy for everything that tries us. The little pot of oil, the Holy Spirit, so faint it may be in His manifested presence that it seems less than the little finger of our hand; but that is the little finger of God, and back of it lies all His omnipotence, wisdom and love. All we have to do is to take that Holy Spirit and pour it into every vessel of need, both for ourselves and others, and the vessels overflow and the blessings only cease when we cease to make room and to pour out.

Look at him again as the sons of the prophet lose their borrowed axe in the river Jordan where they had been cutting wood for their house, and the axe had slipped from the handle to the bottom of the river. Instantly he orders a branch or handle to be dropped into the river. Immediately the axe rises to the surface, and the lost implement is recovered by the hands of the young men.

Smallest and largest emergencies

So our great Prophet is equal to the smallest as well as the largest emergencies. We too lose our axe sometimes—our power for service, our victory over temptation, our peace and joy, our conscious-ness of Christ's presence; but there is a piece of wood—the pilgrim's staff, the sacred promise—that we can ever find equal to the emergency and, as we cast it into the water, our blessing will rise to meet it, our lost axe will come back to us. The very laws of nature may be suspended, the iron can swim again, the thing that was heavier than lead can rise with buoyant wings, the heavy heart can mount above and sing and trust with new power and victory, and we can praise Him whose faithful love has turned darkness into day and sorrow into joy.

Or look again at his triumph over his enemies. The armies of Syria surround him and his servant, and the servant gives a cry of despair, "Alas! my master," as he sees no possible way of escape. All that Elisha asks is that the eyes of his servant may be opened, and on the mountain round about there are armies of angelic horses and chariots and soldiers. Instantly their fears are calmed, and they know that all is well.

So our great Prophet can show us, though every avenue of escape be shut off, that there is ever an upper way that carries us above our foes and a superior host that has the advantage of position over all our enemies.

But that is not all. He asks the Lord to blind the soldiers, and so he goes down to them without a fear and leads them all the way to the city of Samaria. It is indeed a triumph as amusing as it is sublime. When they reach the city, the king is so delighted to have his enemies in his power that he wants to slay them. Elisha treats the proposal as absurd and orders that a magnificent banquet be prepared for them; and so they feed them and feast them until the men are astounded, paralyzed with wonder and dismay at the treatment they have received and when all is over, they are sent back to their own land to tell how easily the prophet of Israel has defeated them without a blow, except from the hand of love. We need hardly wonder when it is added that the bands of the Syrians came no more unto the land of Israel.

And so our great Prophet teaches us to triumph over our foes by the weapons of heavenly love, that the surest way to kill our enemies is by kindness, to consume them by the coals of fire of loving deeds, words and recompenses.

Such is the great and gracious Prophet who is willing to walk by our side, who is willing to dwell in our hearts, to be our wisdom, our guide. Happy are they that walk in His fellowship and in His love! For them no emergency can be extreme, no situation desperate, no adversary formidable. No purpose formed from above can fail. Blessed Prophet, you are ours! Help us to abide in you and follow you evermore!

Isaiah

5. Isaiah, the prophet of high and holy teaching, is the type of Him who leads us into the high and loftiest heights of heavenly truth and life, where the seraphim veil their faces and feet with their wings, and exclaim, "Holy, holy, holy, is the Lord almighty;/ the whole earth is full of his glory" (Isaiah 6:3); where faith mounts up on high to see "the king in his beauty/ and view a land that stretches afar" (33:17); where peace nestles under the shadow of the Rock of Ages; where hope looks out upon His coming, and sings, "The ransomed of the LORD will return./ They will enter Zion with singing;/ everlasting joy will crown their heads./ Gladness and joy will overtake them,/ and sorrow and sighing will flee away" (35:10). "Your sun will never set again; and your moon will wake no more;/ the LORD will be your everlasting light,/ and your days of sorrows will end" (60:20). Holy service waits His power and bidding, and exclaims, " . . . to know the word that sustains the weary./ He wakens me morning by morning,/ wakens my ear to listen like one being taught" (50:4); or, going forth to do His bidding, sings, "How beautiful on

the mountains/ are the feet of those who bring good news,/ who bring good tidings,/ who proclaim salvation,/ who says to Zion,/ 'Your God reigns!' " (52:7). Prayer reaches out in the name of Jesus, with mighty faith, and obeys the great injunction, "Concerning things to come,/ do you question me about my children, or give me orders about the work of my hands?" (45:11b). Holy gladness lifts up its voice and sings, "With joy will you draw water/ from the wells of salvation. . . . Shout aloud and sing for joy, people of Zion,/ for great is the Holy One of Israel among you" (12:3, 6). So still our Prophet speaks to us, teaches us and leads us as we abide in Him.

Daniel

6. Daniel, the prophet of the future, is the type of Him who unfolds to us the vision of His coming and as much of His will for us as it is best for us to know or hope for, for Jesus also shows to us the things to come and leads us into the life of hope as well as of faith and love.

Such is our glorious Prophet. Is He not dearer to us today? Will we not trust Him more fully, follow Him more closely, listen to Him more lovingly and obediently and seek to send abroad His glorious truth among all nations, until the Prophet and the Priest will have become the King of kings and reign from shore to shore?

Making David King

*All these were fighting men who volun-
teered to serve in the ranks. They came
to Hebron fully determined to make
David king over all Israel. All the rest of
the Israelites were also of one mind to
make David king. (1 Chronicles 12:38)*

In one of the chapels of Oxford University there is a beautiful stained glass window, the exterior of which is decorated with sacred pictures from the Old Testament, the interior with corresponding pictures from the New, so that when the sunlight falls upon the window, the two pictures are blended. An observer, standing inside the cathedral, beholds the soft evening light falling upon the picture of Mount Moriah and Abraham's sacrifice of his son Isaac, and at the same time upon the cross of Calvary, which interprets the Old Testament type; or again, perhaps, he will gaze upon the brazen serpent as it blends with the great sacrifice of the Son of Man. Beautifully does this il-

lustrate the connection between the Old Testament
and the New and the glorious fact that all the
scenes of the ancient Scriptures are but figures,
whose full meaning must be learned in the light of
the gospel and the life and death of Jesus Christ!

Of all the Old Testament types of Christ, none is
more remarkable than David—born in Bethlehem,
as Jesus was, a simple shepherd foreshadowing the
great Shepherd, a sufferer and an exile like the
Man of Sorrows, he at length became king and is
preeminently the type of Christ as our great King
and Lord. In this respect he differed from
Solomon, his son. Both of them are types of our
coming King, but Solomon is the type rather of
the kingdom after it will have become established
in peace and righteousness. David, on the contrary,
foreshadows the King of kings in the years and
centuries of His rejection by the world, and as He
slowly conquers His kingdom and wins the crown
which He is to wear with His saints through the
ages of glory.

This is His position today. Like David He has
been anointed and proclaimed the King of the
Church and the nations, but like David He is
rejected by the great majority of mankind, and a
counterfeit king usurps the throne, of whom Saul
was the type. The world today is not subject to the
will of God and the scepter of Jesus and never will
be until He comes a second time. Even the Church
has refused, in large measure, to be subject to her
King, and has allowed the spirit of the world to
control and contaminate her. But the true David

still has His loyal friends and followers, although, like the followers of David in his exile, they are often the humblest of men and yet more and more will be the very outcasts of the world. Their connection with David made them illustrious, and to serve Jesus is enough to dignify and glorify any human name.

Make Christ King

This is the great business of all true Christians today—to make Christ King. Let us first look at the way in which this may be accomplished, and second, at the character of the men on whom He depends to accomplish it, as illustrated in the picture of these ancient worthies who followed the fortunes of David and won for him his crown.

1. Each of us can give Christ the kingdom of our own heart. He will not use us to establish His kingdom in the world until He occupies the throne of our entire being and becomes the King of our affections, our motives, our will and all our heart. This must be done by the full surrender of love—a love that supremely gives Him the highest place and makes Him our all in all. The ancient Pantheon offered a niche to the Christians for the image of Jesus, but they answered, "Our God must reign alone; we can have but one king, and Christ must be the sovereign of all our hearts." He is preparing today a people for His glory, and this is to be the test, that they follow the Lamb wherever He goes and give Him the bridal love that displaces every other which could for a moment hinder His

supremacy. Have you given Christ all your heart, and so you gladly do it now? The answer of your consciousness is the best test of your consecration.

2. You can take Christ as the King of your life by giving Him your difficulties and adversaries to overcome and permitting Him to subdue all His enemies and yours and reign as Lord of all. Everything that comes up in your life is but another opportunity of giving Him a larger and richer crown. It is too strong for you, but not for Him. Your land of promise is not a luxurious inheritance of self-indulgent ease, but a battlefield of countless foes and ever harder, nobler triumphs. Every confederacy of hostile kings that comes up to meet you is but another challenge to prove the might of your great Captain and all-conquering King. Instead of shrinking and complaining that the conflict is so hard and the foes so mighty and so many, you should recognize them as His foes rather than yours and hand them over to Him for still more glorious victories.

It was of the Lord that those kings should have come against Joshua with the intent that they might be utterly destroyed. Every son of Anak that marched out against the armies of Israel was sent forth at God's command not to destroy Israel, but to meet their own destruction; and but for the battle there never could have been the annihilation of the foe. And so he says to us, "without being frightened in any way by those who oppose you. This is a sign to them that they will be destroyed, but that you will be saved—and that by God"

(Philippians 1:28). Nothing ever comes up in your life but Christ anticipated it long ago, has been prepared for it from the beginning, and, if you will let Him, will carry you through it in glorious victory. This is the meaning of His kingdom; He is thus winning for you and Himself a mutual crown. Will you exalt Him over all your difficulties and trials and crown Him Lord of all?

3. We can make Christ King by laboring for the evangelization of the world and the spread of His glorious truth and work. We can win for Him the crown of many hearts and thus hasten His glorious coming.

Two ways

There are two ways especially in which this can be done. The first is in calling out His bride even from the Church; not necessarily in the sense of separating them from the communion of the Church, but rather in the sense of separating them unto Him in entire consecration. He is preparing for Himself a bride, not consisting of mere professors, but of those who are wholly His, separated from the world and sin, robed in the whitest garments of His perfect righteousness and wedded in affection to Him alone as their Bridegroom and Lord.

We can accomplish this by spreading the gospel among the unsaved and sending it out especially to the heathen world. The great call of the Master today is to the evangelization of the nations; and when this has been accomplished, there will be no barrier in the way of His immediate return. Are we thus laboring to make Christ King, spreading His glorious truth and calling all nations to prepare for His millennial reign? This is the real purpose of God for His church today; not so much to build up great and permanent institutions, as to be a messenger of the glad tidings and to publish among the nations the glorious news that the King is about to come.

Napoleon, in his hour of pride, refused to receive a crown from human hands, but, taking in his own fingers the royal diadem and placing it upon his head, he exclaimed, "These hands have won; these hands alone shall give the crown of empire." But the Lord Jesus desires to receive His crown from those who love Him and honors us with the great privilege of winning it for Him and laying it at His dear feet. The Lord help us to hasten His kingdom and to add to the glory of His many crowns!

Those who make Him King

1. David's men had all been unhappy, helpless, and indeed, we might say, worthless, for we read that whosoever was in debt or in any kind of trouble resorted to David in the cave of Adullam, and David made them one of his mighty men. Before they came to him they were the outlaws of society, but the moment they touched David they became ennobled and afterwards were raised to be his princes and the officers of the kingdom. Even so we, whom Christ has chosen as His friends and fellow-workers, are by nature poor, unworthy sin-

ners, with nothing to recommend us but simply this—that we have followed Jesus and that He has touched us with His royal hand; and this is enough to make us glorious and illustrious. Sinners by nature and practice, we have been washed in His precious blood. Our love to Him is accepted as better than royal blood, and by-and-by He will say to us,

> You are those who have stood by me in my trials. And I confer on you a kingdom, just as my Father conferred one on me, so that you may eat and drink at my table in my kingdom and sit on thrones, judging the twelve tribes of Israel. (Luke 22:28–30)

2. In the description of the respective tribes that came up to make David king, we read of the Benjamites (1 Chronicles 12:2), that "they were armed with bows and were able to shoot arrows or to sling stones right-handed or left-handed." They were two-handed men, i.e., all their power was given to their master and they were ready, not only in season, but out of season, for service and warfare. So Christ would have His true soldiers not only speak out of a pulpit or to read from a manuscript, but ever prepared to speak a word of warning or comfort or salvation as opportunity requires.

3. They were armed men. They were "able to handle the shield and [buckler, KJV]. Their faces were the faces of lions, and they were as swift as gazelles in the mountains" (8). There is a dif-

ference between a shield and a buckler. A shield is something that you yourself hold, but a buckler is something that is fastened upon the arm and that cannot be lost. There is a kind of faith that we cling to, and there is a faith that holds us and that we cannot lose—even the faith of God—like the buckler on the arm which we retain in the heat of battle and which even the dying warrior still holds above his chest. This is the faith that Christ would have us receive and in which He would have us conquer.

4. They were courageous men; they feared no danger. "It was they who crossed the Jordan in the first month when it was overflowing all its banks, and they put to flight everyone living in the valleys, to the east and to the west" (15). They had a hard test. As they approached the Jordan there were enemies upon the east, but they scattered them like the smoke before the wind. Next, the Jordan had flooded its banks and could not be forded, but they sprang into the flood and swam across, fearing neither flood nor foe. When they reached the farther shore, still the enemy stood facing them along the banks, but they put them to flight. Perhaps they did not even wait for the battle, for men so brave were not likely to meet a formidable resistance. And when we press through the tides of opposition and the hosts of hell, we will find our enemies still encamped before us, and each battle will be on the verge of a greater victory still to come.

5. They were true-hearted men.

David went out to meet them and said to them, "If you have come to me in peace, to help me, I am ready to have you unite with me. But if you have come to betray me to my enemies when my hands are free from violence, may the God of our fathers see it and judge you."

Then the Spirit came upon Amasai, chief of the Thirty, and he said:

"We, are yours, O David!
    We are with you, O son of Jesse!
Success, success to you,
    and success to those who help you,
        for your God will help you." (17–18)

So Christ wants loyal friends; loyal not only to Him, but loyal to His people too. Their cry was not only, "success to you," but "success to those who help you."

6. Next, they were wise men. "Men of Issachar, who understood the times and knew what Israel should do" (32). And so our King wants wise men today; men that do not waste their strength in misguided efforts, men that are not fighting over old issues long since obsolete or beating the air with mere speculations and theories that have no practical bearing. He wants men of today that understand the Lord's meaning for our times and catch His thought for their generation, and are living for the work of the present hour. Such men, like the men of Issachar, have all their brethren at their command and exert the sacred influences that con-

trol their minds and make them leaders of the great hosts of God.

7. They were men that could "keep rank" (verse 33, KJV). That is, they were adjustable and congenial men who could work in cooperation with others; not narrow, bigoted and impracticable people, with whom nobody could work, as Christians sometimes are, but large-hearted, loving, humble workers, who knew their places, who took any place, who were not afraid to take the lowest place, who could obey orders as well as give them, who could walk in fellowship with other soldiers, who could keep step with other soldiers and maintain the unbroken rank in the host of God. God give us this spirit! The nearer we are to God the less angular we will be, and the easier it will be to work with us.

8. Again, they were single-hearted men (verse 33). They were able "to help David with undivided loyalty." Their whole heart was with David. Their whole interest was invested in his kingdom. Their whole being was given to his honor and advancement. And so we cannot be true soldiers for Christ unless we have given Him all our heart; and nothing can separate us from Him when we are utterly devoted to His honor and interest, every other attachment and every other interest being subject to His highest will and glory and eternally linked with His kingdom. We cannot have our heart in the world that has no interest in Him and on things that must perish, but every part of our being must be invested in His coming and His glory.

This is also the meaning of the perfect heart referred to in verse 38. God give us such a spirit in the blessed work of hastening the coming of our blessed Lord!

We are passing through the days of David's suffering and humiliation. He is not yet upon the throne of this world, although He has the right to reign and a sure decree has been passed in heaven. "I have installed my King/ on Zion, my holy hill" (Psalm 2:6). But He is now in the days of His obscurity, and the badge of His service is a cross and a crown. He is passing through the world and picking out His future princes, testing them by their loyal devotion to His person and will. Oh, that we all may be true in these days and honored with a part of the glory in that day.

An illustration

It is said that the great Ivan of Russia used to go among his people in disguise and test them. One night he went through the suburbs of his capital and knocked at many lowly cabins as a poor, wandering tramp, asking for a night's lodging and a crust of bread. He was refused from door to door, until at last he came to a humble cabin where a poor man was attending his wife and newborn babe. He opened the door at the knock of the wanderer, kindly invited him in, treated him with courtesy and attention, gave him a crude bed and a humble supper and bade him goodnight with great kindness. The emperor lay, sleeping little and thinking much, and in the early morning he took his leave amid many thanks. Late in the afternoon the royal chariot drove to the door and halted. The poor man fled to the gate in great alarm, prostrated himself at the feet of his emperor and asked him if he had committed any crime to cause his displeasure. The emperor assured him it was all right, and then added, "I have simply come to thank you for your kindness to your emperor last night. He came in the disguise of a beggar to test your love, and now he comes as your sovereign to reward your loyalty. This bag of gold is for your newborn child. As he grows up I will adopt him as my child and will give him a place of high and honorable service in the empire, and if I can be of any service to you and yours, command your emperor."

So Christ is passing by today. He is coming soon. The Lord help us to know Him and receive Him in His lowliness, and may ours be the joy in that day of receiving His smile and recognition in the midst of a dissolving world and a despairing multitude!

Christ Our Head

And he is the head of the body, the church; he is the beginning and the firstborn from among the dead, so that in everything he might have the supremacy. For God was pleased to have all his fullness dwell in him. (Colossians 1:18–19)

The human body is the paragon and crown of the material universe. It was the last thing that God ever created, and so satisfied was He with His glorious work that He chose this wondrous and beautiful temple for His own abode and has made the form of man forevermore the embodiment of His own eternal Son. The fact that Jesus Christ is incarnate in a body like our own has placed humanity on the pinnacle of creation and the throne of God. Forever and forever a wondering universe will come to behold their God and will see Him in a form like yours and mine. It is little wonder, therefore, that this exquisite workmanship of God should be worthy of the honor and dignity conferred upon it, and should show in all its structures the works of infinite wisdom, power and love. Even David, long before the study of physiology had revealed the wonders of the human frame, could say, "I will praise you because I am fearfully and wonderfully made" (Psalm 139:14a). How much more profound the wonder and praise that should fill our hearts as the progress of human knowledge enables us to understand better the exquisite and infinite skill displayed in the creation of a single member of our body!

Perhaps the most striking evidence of Christianity ever presented in Christian literature was the Bridgewater treatise on the human hand, showing the delicate mechanism of the numerous bones, nerves, vessels and the varied and perfect functions of the various parts of even that little member. How much more delicate and perfect the structure of the human brain and the relation of the head to all the physical organism of the vital functions! This is the figure which the apostle uses to express the relation of Jesus Christ to His people and their mutual relationship to Him as the body of Christ. May His Spirit enable us to apply the beautiful figure in such a way that we will be drawn closer to our living Head and to one another in Him!

Seat of will and authority

1. In the human body the head is the *seat of will and authority*. The body is obedient to its voli-

tions, and these commands are so instructive that
the body obeys without an effort. It is perfectly
natural to follow the wishes of the head. So the
Lord Jesus Christ, our living Head, is the true Lord
and sovereign of His people's lives, and it is the
place of their bodies to be instinctively obedient to
His every wish. If He is indeed our Head, it will be
our second nature to do His bidding. Indeed, no
other part of the body has any power to will, and
none of Christ's children should have any will
apart from their Master's. There is a great difference between being guided by your own head or
somebody else's. If Christ is not your living Head,
you will not want His authority and government.
Therefore, before we can truly obey Him, we must
fully receive Him and be so united with Him that
His interests are ours and His will is just the expression of our inmost being.

Source and seat of life

2. In the human body the head is the *source and
seat of life*, and so the Lord Jesus is the source of
His people's life. There is no life apart from the
head, and we have none apart from Him. Our
regeneration comes through the quickening power
of His life; our sanctification is His indwelling in
us. Our physical life may be made manifest in the
flesh. We are dependent upon Him for our fruit, for
our joy, for our love, for all our spiritual grace and
experiences, and He loves to impart His life to us
and fill us more abundantly if we will but receive
it. We are not held responsible for our own life. We

are not expected to manufacture either faith or love, but receive from Him life and love and the grace that He is ever longing to impart.

Source of sensation

3. The head is the *source of sensation*. All feeling comes from the brain and resides in it. When you hurt your hand it is not your hand that feels, but your head, although it seems to be in your members. What a beautiful parable of the sympathy of our living Head! Every sorrow and pain we feel is instinctively telegraphed to Him and touches His living heart to the quick. "For we do not have a high priest who is unable to sympathize with our weaknesses" (Hebrews 4:15a). When Paul was outraging the saints of God and compelling them to blaspheme the name of Jesus under penalty of death, the voice of the Master called to him from heaven, "Saul, Saul, why do you persecute me?" (Acts 9:4b). He was hurting, not others, but the Master's head. The heavenly Head was suffering for the earthly members. The hurt hand was communicating its pain to the Head in heaven. How quickly the head sends relief to the suffering hand or foot! Have you ever noticed when you receive a blow or are pierced with a thorn, how quickly all the blood in the body rushes to the injured place, and it flushes with a crimson tide? It simply means that the brain has become concerned for the suffering member and has ordered all the resources of the system on duty, and every drop of blood in the body is coursing to the sore place to give it a touch

of relief. What you call an inflammation is just the effort of nature through increased circulation to lave away the intruding pain and stimulate and quicken the system to throw it off.

So Christ is ever nearest the sad heart, the tempted child, the wandering one, and all the resources of His grace are at our service in every time of need.

When Margaret Wilson was standing tied to a stake on Solway Beach, waiting for the tide to come in and take her martyred life, her persecutors placed an older saint farther down the beach that little Margaret might see the saintly woman die before her turn should come, and thus be dissuaded by terror from bold testimony to Jesus. But as the cruel waves leaped on Margaret McLaughlin and trampled out her life, and the rough soldier by Margaret Wilson's side asked, hoping to turn her back from her purpose even at the last, "What do you think of that?" She meekly answered, "I think I see Christ in one of His members suffering there." How beautiful! How true!

When the pressure seems intolerable, when sorrow gnaws the heart, when Satan hurls his arrows of flame into our quivering spirit, when the world opposes us as it once did Him, and flesh and heart are ready to faint and fail, it is just Christ in one of His members suffering there. The living Head will not fail nor forget to help the suffering member.

All sensation must come from the brain, and so all spiritual feeling must come from Christ. Let us not, therefore, try to work up our feelings, but

keep close to Him, and the tides of His love will
flow into our consciousness and spiritual sen-
sibilities. The secret of joy and love will spring
within us from the Head. The most artless and
spontaneous life will ever be the best. Oftentimes
He may wish us to be quiescent. Let us be acquies-
cent in this, and when He rests in His love, let us
rest with Him, and when He rejoices over us with
singing, let us swell the chorus in glad responses,
our hearts keeping time to His, as the sand upon
the ocean shore is wet or dry as the ocean tide rises
and falls in the sea below.

The seat of power

4. The head is the *seat of power*, and so Christ is
His people's power. We are not strong in ourselves,
but He is our strength. "All authority in heaven
and on earth has been given to me. . . . And surely I
am with you always" (Matthew 28:18b, 20b). We
will receive the power of the Holy Ghost coming
upon us. This, therefore, is the secret of effective
service. You will always feel your own lack of
power; but as you go forth obedient to the orders
of the Head, the Head will follow up your obedient
steps and render effectual your service. Christ
never sends His people on any ministry without
equipping them, sustaining them and rendering
their work effectual. Your usefulness does not
depend upon natural gifts or conditions, but upon
your closeness to your Head.

A very humble Christian ever filled with Jesus
will so speak, so look, so grasp your hand, so do

the commonest things of life, that strange and everlasting forces will spring from the act and touch hearts on every side. A very small wire filled with electricity will make everybody conscious of strange power.

It is a glorious and mighty thing to stand among men and be conscious that you have the authority and power of the Almighty, and that He is charging your message with a weight and responsibility which will meet those men in the judgment and which will move and influence their whole earthly life whether they hear or whether they forbear.

Seat of thought

5. The head is the *seat of thought, intelligence, judgment, direction, knowledge*. So Christ is our wisdom, our guide, our mind. We need not think so much, or rather He will think His thoughts in us if we suspend our judgment and draw upon His glorious mind for our knowledge, our light, our views, our opinions and plans. It is not the business of the hand to be planning and thinking, but simply to go forward at the bidding of the brain. So He has said to us, "Do not worry about your life . . . your heavenly Father knows that you need them" (Mathew 6:25a, 32b). "Cast all your anxiety on him because he cares for you" (1 Peter 5:7).

Seat of honor, glory and beauty

6. The head is the *seat of honor, glory and beauty*. It supports the lovely face; it crowns the glorious temple. It is borne aloft in dignity and

majesty, and in all things has the preeminence. It wears the crown of royalty, or the wreath of beauty, and is the expression and embodiment of dignity and preeminence. So Jesus Christ is the glory of His people, the crowned Head of His church to whom alone belong all dominion, praise and love forever and ever. To Him, not to us, belongs the honor. He is our Head and our glory, and He forever shall receive the many crowns of all His dear ones whose joy it will be to lay them at His feet or heap them upon His head. All His richest blessings must lead us from them to Him. All His dearest children must be but links and channels to lift our hearts to Him from whom comes all love and all loveliness in earth or heaven.

The Body

The body is as necessary as the head. A bodiless head would be as abnormal as a headless body, and so our blessed Lord needs us as much as we need Him. He has separated Himself from His old place of absolute Deity and chosen for His inheritance His people, and without them His life is incomplete. All the gifts that He has received from the Father need an outlet, and we are the channels through whom they find expression and development. His love to men, His purpose to redeem them, His grace and power can only reach them through our intervention. When we are not at His bidding and open to His influence, He is paralyzed in His purpose and baffled in His designs. It is like a man whose brain is full of magnificent energy and purpose, whose heart is throbbing with boundless love, but whose limbs are paralyzed and whose hands are limp and dead, his body refusing to perform the wishes of his brain and clogging and depressing him with its helplessness, his love all vain because of the want of harmony and the lack of correspondence between the body and the head.

Christ has been hindered by the paralyzed, disjointed, diseased condition of many members of His body, and the work accomplished by the Church has been limited by the fact that the body has been diseased and enfeebled in many of its parts. Oh, what might not be realized in a few days for the accomplishment of redemption if the entire body of Christ, without an exception, were open to the love of the Head and obedient to all His wishes and will. Pentecost would be repeated with a multiplication as vast as the difference between the 120 millions of Christians today and the 120 brethren in the upper room. There are millions of times as many members in the body today as there were then, but the very number restrains the body all the more when they are not perfectly adjustable and responsive to the Head. Will you remember, beloved, that Jesus needs you and that even if you are the weakest and smallest member, you have the power by becoming diseased and inflamed to spread disease through the whole body, even as the smallest finger on your hand can paralyze your hand by simply getting sick and sore?

Three things especially are emphasized by the

apostle in his beautiful teaching about the body of Christ.

Its variety

1. "The body is a unit, though it is made up of many parts; and though all its parts are many, they form one body. So it is with Christ" (1 Corinthians 12:12). In your body there are thousands of constituent elements. Every one is necessary. The very diversity of those members is your strength. Members of the church of Christ are not all alike. The greater the diversity, the more their power. Each of us has our natural individuality, and this is the element through which God molds our spiritual life and our life plans. He has made each of us for a certain place and service, and the very things that constitute our personal identity are the things He wants to use in us.

Sometimes our very eccentricities are elements of force when consecrated to God and baptized with the Holy Ghost. Sometimes the very facts of your previous history, even your sins and errors, become features which God can utilize for His kingdom. Do not, therefore, criticize your peculiarities. They are the very things God wants, if they are not defects. Your very littleness may just fit you for the place He wants you to fill. In making up a body He sometimes only wants a finger or a single hair. Now if you were a thumb or a glowing eye, you would be needless, because, you see, there are enough of these already, and you are just required to fit into your place and functions. Do not

criticize in others their idiosyncrasies, as you are
pleased to call them, for in the body there are some
curious members. The apostle says that those that
have least honor, to them God has given more
abundant honor, and the time often comes when
those obscure and uncongenial persons become,
perhaps, the greatest blessings of your life and
draw you to them as the Lord Himself.

Its unity

2. These diversities may all be blended and kept
by a common bond of love and life in Jesus. If completely united, the very diversity adds greatly to the
scope and influence of the church of Christ. On the
field of Gettysburg a little pool of blood was found
into which flowed fine tiny streams, and when the
men from whose wounds the life tides were issuing
were found, they proved to be the sons of different
races, so that in that little crimson pool the heart
of a German, a Frenchman, an Irishman and an
African were all blending; and it had but one color
and one meaning, the love of country that was not
afraid to die. If Christ's love is in our heart, all differences become small. A creed will not unite us; a
work will not unite us; a love, and a love only, can
unite us. Closeness to Jesus brings closeness to
each other. The little birdlings that are always
nestling against the mother's bosom are always
pushing against each other, and if you and I are
determined to be nearer to Jesus, we will never be
far apart. A lack of unity in the body is fatal to
health and power. An obstructive joint will bring

rheumatism and paralysis. The reason today that the power of the Holy Ghost is so limited is because the interflow and the outway of the life of Christ are hindered by the divisions of Christianity, and still more by the lack of heart-oneness to Him.

Its relationship

3. We owe to each other certain mutual obligations expressed by the phrase, "joined and held together by every supporting ligament" (Ephesians 4:16a). While every member of the body sustains a relationship in some sense to every other, yet some are closer than others. In those intimate relationships there must be perfect freedom, fellowship and holy activity. The joint and the socket must move together without friction. The least friction will produce inflammation, irritation, pain, disease, paralysis. God adjusts us to each other by His Providence and Spirit, and He will enable us to recognize our relationships, to meet them, and fulfill them perfectly with holy wisdom and love. Each of us sustains many relationships, but the Holy Spirit in us will adjust us to each with a perfect freedom and delicacy, so that we will love one another in Christ in the places where we belong with a heart as free as heaven and as pure as Christ Himself. You will have a boundless love for each of God's children, each in his place. You will love your family, your children, your friends, your brother in Christ, each in his or her place with perfect simplicity of heart, and yet without a jar in the various relationships. For if Christ is abiding in us

He will adjust to every relationship even as He Himself meets each of us, His members, with the fullness of His heart, and yet the special adaption of each one is what their situation requires.

The recognizing of our oneness with Christ will make us considerate of one another and will give to our duty to each other a higher sacredness, inasmuch as it affects the whole body and the Head Himself. When you hinder or hurt a single brother, you hurt the whole body just the same as in your physical body where a jar in one part will hinder the rest of the body. And not only so, you will come to recognize the necessity of being right with God, for otherwise you may hinder the entire work of Christ.

It is not necessary for a man to be sick all over to be helpless; a single organ will render him helpless. And so, if you choose, you can, by becoming an irritation and an offense, arrest and obstruct all God's work to a certain extent. Of course, there is provision in the human body for getting rid of such a member, and sometimes the only thing is to cut it off.

God has the same provision for His Church, and He will separate you from His people if you are not willing to work with them in harmony and holiness. And yet excision always leaves a scar and often a lack. The law of love and the desire of the Master is that we should be so true to Him and to each other that He can accomplish in us and through us His highest purposes of love and blessing. It will help us infinitely in our relationship with people to recognize them in Christ and not in themselves. Then our love to them will not be personal and selfish, but will be heavenly and holy. Then also we shall be enabled to love what naturally we could not even tolerate.

Recognize the mystery

Oh, we little know the depths and heights of joy and power that lie hidden in recognizing the mystery of the body of Christ, and Christ Himself in all His members! Then our service will be all unto Him, and a cup of cold water given to a disciple for Jesus' sake will bring a great reward, and some day the Master will say, "You did [it] for me." Then also it will be found that the simplest and humblest services have been of the greatest value, even as the poor old widow in ancient Constantinople, who could only sprinkle the grass upon the rough stones as they dragged them to the temple, is represented in the old legend as having her name inscribed on the front of the Cathedral in letters of gold traced by an angel's hand, "This house the widow Eudoxia built to God."

Then also will we know the exceeding joy of doing much of our work through others, and doing the rest almost unconsciously and impersonally until the day comes when He will trace each constituent and give to each his proportionate reward. I am so glad to feel that in that day most of my work for the Lord will be rewarded to others who have helped me oftentimes by sprinkling grass for the rough stones and making it

easier where it would have been so hard, but for
the love and prayers of God's dear children. God is
preparing His Church for the most glorious spec-
tacle the universe has ever beheld, in that crown-
ing day when the whole of creation will be
summoned to gaze upon the face of the bride, the
Lamb's wife. As they gaze they will see not only the
face of the Bride in all the beauty of her myriad-
fold individuality, but as the unity and light of all
the phases of the Lamb Himself reflected in them
all, and, while it will be a picture of glorified
humanity, it will be still more a picture of the Son
of Man.

A dear friend has given me this beautiful illustration suggested by a single painting. Here is a
woman's face. It is loveliness itself as its features
are traced upon the canvas in the soft, vivid light of
Italian art. There is the perfect form, the warm
color, the modest yet noble brow, the rich tresses
of hair, the expression of loveliness, the repose and
strength of character, all seeming to speak with
the light of life itself. Such is the picture as you see
it at a distance, but when you come a little closer a
strange transformation takes place. Making up that
one face you see a hundred other faces and objects,
and you find that it is a composite painting made
up of many minutiae, so shaded and compounded
that at a distance the combined effect was that of a
single face, but at closer inspection it is a cluster of
many objects. There, forming the rich color of the
lips, are exquisitely shaded flowers; the hair is
formed of trailing vines and grasses; little faces of

beautiful children fit into the countenance; rich clusters of fruit the eye; and all blended together in infinite diversity and yet perfect unison.

Such will be the face that this universe will yet behold—Jesus, shining in all, All in all. Your face will be there, in perfect identity, and yet blended in the soft light of His countenance and reflecting the radiance of His smile. So let us abide in Him and grow up together into Him until we will see the fullness of the stature of Christ Jesus.

CHAPTER
10

Our Horn of Salvation

Praise be to the Lord, the God of Israel,/ because he has come and has redeemed his people./ He has raised up a horn of salvation for us/ in the house of his servant David/ (as he said through his holy prophets of long ago),/ salvation from our enemies and from the hand of all who hate us—/to show mercy to our fathers and to remember his holy covenant,/ the oath he swore to our father Abraham:/ to rescue us from the hand of our enemies,/ and to enable us to serve him without fear/ in holiness and righteousness before him all our days. (Luke 1:68–75)

Zechariah, the father of John the Baptist and the author of this song, was practically the last of the priesthood. Because of his priestly office he was chosen to be the father of John the Baptist, and thus, both directly and through his son, the witness to Christ, although Judaism afterwards rejected Christ notwithstanding its own testimony. True to the spirit of Judaism, when the message came to Zechariah about the birth of his son, his unbelief refused to accept it, and God visited him with dumbness and silence until the birth of John. The silence of Zechariah was significant of the silence that was to fall on Judaism as she gave place to the testimony of Christ and sank back into silence at His feet, while all heaven proclaimed, "This is my Son, whom I love; . . . Listen to Him!" (Matthew 17:5b).

How different was the spirit of Mary when the message came to her requiring even greater faith! More truly she represented the spirit of Christianity. She implicitly believed it, and her answer was, "I am the Lord's servant, . . . May it be to me as you have said" (Luke 1:38).

But at length Zechariah's lips were opened at the circumcision of his son, and with this last song his voice died away with the voice of Judaism into eternal silence. There is a beautiful bird which has but one song, and that its own death dirge. After silently sailing the waters for its whole life long, the beautiful swan at last, on the bosom of some peaceful lake, perhaps as the shadows of evening are falling and darkness is passing over its simple brain, opens its mouth and pours out the strangest, saddest song that ever fell upon the ear. Then its beautiful, graceful neck relaxes and it sinks upon the waves in the silence of death. It has breathed its life out in its one last song. So

Zechariah passes out of view with his own song, but it was a song worthy to be lost in, for it is the keynote of redemption and yet will re-echo in the song of Moses and the Lamb. There are three strains in it. Like all great songs, it is extremely simple, but swells out into infinite echoes of glory and blessing.

He has visited His people

We love to receive a letter from a friend, but how much more the friend himself! Sweet is the message of affection, but sweeter the visit of our loved ones! The glory of Zechariah's song was that God was about to visit His people. This was the cry of Moses, "If your Presence does not go with us, do not send us up from here. How will anyone know that you are pleased with me and with your people unless you go with us? What else will distinguish me and your people from all the other people on the face of the earth?" (Exodus 33:15–16). Not even an angel's presence would satisfy or fill the place, none but God Himself. This was the burden of all Isaiah's promises. The Lord Himself will come to visit His people. This is the preeminent glory of redemption. God Himself has undertaken it. The Eternal One has come to our world in person and identified Himself forever with humanity.

It tells the story of the incarnation. "The Word became flesh and made his dwelling among us. We have seen his glory, the glory of the One and Only, who came from the Father, full of grace and truth" (John 1:14). He has come into our house of clay, and He has come to stay and to the latest ages of eternity. Generation after generation will visit the universe, lift up their eyes to look upon God and see the face of a man, a form like our own, God in the likeness of humanity. He has come so near to us that He has come into our own nature.

> Since the children have flesh and blood, he too shared in their humanity so that by his death he might destroy him who holds the power of death—that is, the devil . . . For surely it is not angels he helps, but Abraham's descendants. For this reason he had to be made like his brothers in every way, in order that he might become a merciful and faithful high priest in service to God. (Hebrews 2:14–17a)

When the first missionaries went to St. Thomas, they could not get near the suffering and degraded slaves until they took part in their bondage and asked the masters to make them slaves also. Then they were received with perfect confidence and were able to bring multitudes of the poor suffering ones to Christ. They trusted them when they saw that they had become identified with their very own life and lot. "Praise be to the Lord the God of Israel,/ because he has come and has redeemed his people" (Luke 1:68).

But He comes closer. These missionaries could work by the side of the slave, but they could not come into their hearts. I can sit down and talk with

you in your home, but I cannot walk into your
brain and into your spirit and put my being into
yours so that you will have my thoughts and feelings and life. In some measure love can impart almost its own soul to the beloved one, and yet only
in a faint measure compared with the great and
divine example which Christ has forever set before
us; for He not only has visited our race, but He has
visited our hearts, and made our very bodies His
temple and home.

> For this is what the high and lofty One says—
> he who lives forever, whose name is holy:
> "I live in a high and holy place,
> but also with him who is contrite and lowly
> in spirit." (Isaiah 57:15a)

> I will put my dwelling place among you, . . . I
> will walk among you and be your God, and
> you will be my people. (Leviticus 26:11–12)

Has He visited you, beloved? Has He come into
your brain and possessed all its thoughts and given
to you His light and wisdom, His understanding
and mind? Has He come into your will and taken
the key of the chamber from which all the acts and
purposes of your lives are directed? Has He been
admitted to the innermost chamber of your confidences, where only your dearest ones ever come?
Does He control all your heart's affections and
supremely hold them for Himself, so that you have
no life apart from Him? Has He found his way

without restraint into every inmost apartment until you find they are being enlarged by His ministry and filled in every capacity with His love and life, as He thinks in you, trusts in you, wills in you, rejoices in you, speaks in you, prays in you, praises in you and pours out through your whole being the fullness of His life—not a transient visitor, but a perpetual Guest? Oh! how much He will do for the heart that thus receives Him!

Happy was the loving woman of Shunem the day that Elisha passed her door that she received him in the name of the Lord and made him welcome to her home and her heart. Little did she dream that it was going to bring her, in the coming years, deliverance from her sorrows and her trials, the child of her affection, and that child a second time restored from death itself.

What care He will take of the house that He owns and lives in! How He will love to heal, strengthen, beautify and glorify the temple of His indwelling. What infinite rest it is to live with Christ in His own house, and have Him bear all the burdens and responsibilites, while you dwell a happy guest in the house you once called your own.

A more glorious visit

And then He is coming in a little while on a still more glorious visit, with sound of trumpet and mighty processions of angels and ransomed men, while earth and heaven will signal His glorious advent by signs and wonders such as the universe has never beheld.

The King of kings is passing by these days of
time, a lowly man and a wayfarer. He asks a
sacrifice of you. He asks a welcome from you. He
asks the key of your heart's inmost chamber. Will
you trust Him? The day is coming when it will be
much to have one glance from His glorious face, to
have Him recognize you among the myriads of the
resurrection and say, "Come my little child, and sit
with me on my throne, and share my kingdom; for
on earth you received me, and even so do I now
welcome you."

Yes, He is coming again to visit our earth and to
leave it no more. "Now the dwelling of God is with
men," will be the announcement of that glad day,
"and he will live with them . . . and God himself
will be with them" (Revelation 21:3). "They will see
his face, and his name will be on their foreheads.
There will be no more night" (22:4–5a).

Even when the glad millennial age is ended, it
will expand into a gladder and better time, and the
new heavens will be added to the new earth.
Redeemed humanity will colonize over all this
great universe, and we may have stars for
kingdoms and worlds for our inheritance. Then
will we sing as we cannot now, "Praise be to the
Lord, the God of Israel, because he has come and
has redeemed his people" (Luke 1:68).

He has redeemed His people

This is much more. The missionary can stoop to
the lowly condition of the slaves, but he cannot set
them free. He can die with them in their chains,

but he cannot break the fetters. Jesus not only visited His people, but He has redeemed them. He has given His own freedom for ours, and the ransom suffices, and the great manifesto has gone forth. "The Spirit of the Sovereign Lord is on me,/ because the Lord has anointed me/ to preach good news to the poor. . . . to proclaim freedom for the captives" (Isaiah 61:1). This word redeemed is the characteristic term of the gospel. It speaks of the crimson tint of sin and the deeper crimson of Calvary's blood. It tells of a heaven that has cost something, a salvation that is established on the eternal principles of justice and righteousness that has met every claim of law and right, and that has placed the ransomed soul in as good a position as if he had never sinned.

All human hearts instinctively know that such a redemption was demanded. The most stone age savage is conscious that some propitation must be made for sin and that evil cannot be lightly passed over, even by clemency, without some satisfaction. When the proud and haughty Tarquin sat upon the bench to judge his own son, with the Roman instincts of justice, he could not acquit him. When the mother pleaded for her boy with bitter tears, and brothers and sisters claimed his life, and the citizens who loved him interceded, the father could only answer, "The father loves him as much as you, but the judge must punish him," and to the lictors he was delivered without mercy, to be beaten and slain because law and justice could know no mercy.

Very beautifully have the Hindu legends embodied this truth, and at the same time foreshadowed the mystery of the gospel through which love has triumphed over justice and yet has left justice uncompromised and vindicated.

In the ancient Hindu legends there is a story of a poor sinner pursued by the spirit of retribution in the form of a demon. Flying from its pursuer and about to be overtaken, the sinful spirit cried to Vishnu, the goddess of Mercy, for help, and she immediately changed the fugitive into a dove.

With a glad cry of gratitude the dove swept up into the air, striking her wings upon the firmament and bore away above her pursuer, thanking her kind deliverer. But a moment later the demon had been changed into a hawk, and she found herself pursued by a stronger wing and a swifter flight than her own.

She was about to be struck down by the cruel talons of the hawk when suddenly she lifted up her prayer again to Vishnu, and the goddess opened her bosom as an asylum for the fluttering dove and folded her wings about her as she lay there secure from her enemy.

Then the hawk approached the goddess and demanded his prey. "She is mine," he said, "by every right of justice. You, Vishnu, have declared and know that sin must be punished and that I am entitled to my victim, and I demand her life or its equivalent."

Vishnu answered, "I recognize your claim. Her life you cannot have, but you may have as much of mine as will be its equivalent." And with that she opened her bosom to the devourer and bade him thrust his fierce beak and talons into her quivering flesh until he had torn from her breast as much as he would have consumed if he had devoured the little dove.

Satisfied, he withdrew, and the trembling dove looked upon the bleeding breast and knew what its life had cost its deliverer. And as it floated away a little later with the stain of blood upon its wings, it never could forget what its redemption had meant.

You and I were that dove. Justice pursued us with every claim of right. Even God could not forego its claim, but must execute it or cease to be God. But the blessed Redeemer opened His bosom, gave His life and blood to meet the claim, bore the judgment we deserved, and now sprinkled with this precious blood, we sing,

> To him who loves us and has freed us from our sins by his blood . . . be glory and power for ever and ever! (Revelation 1:6)

> Worthy is the Lamb, who was slain. (5:12a)

> And with your blood you purchased men for God/ . . . You have made them to be a kingdom and priests to serve our God. (5:9b–10a)

> Praise be to the Lord, the God of Israel,/ because he has come and has redeemed his people. (Luke 1:68)

He has raised up a horn of salvation

Salvation is the fruition of redemption. Redemption purchases it, salvation realizes it and brings it into our actual experience. Zechariah speaks not so much of salvation as of the "horn of salvation." This bold figure, perhaps, originated in primitive times when mighty hunters, like Nimrod, returning from the chase, loved to grace their tents with the splendid horns of the animals that they had slain: the antlers of the deer, the tusks of the elephant, and the horn, perhaps, of the mighty rhinoceros. And so the word "horn" came to be the figure of beauty, power and dominion. It has passed into the imagery of inspired prophecy and song, so that we find the earthly powers described by Daniel and John as horns upon the head of the beast.

And so we find the Psalmist speaking of God as his Horn of Salvation and his High Tower. In speaking, therefore, of Christ as a Horn of Salvation, Zechariah meant to emphasize the glory and beauty of the Savior, His supreme and universal dominion and His infinite and divine power. It is Coronation, singing, "Bring forth the royal diadem, and crown Him Lord of all." The verse that follows explains this thought more perfectly than any words of ours can do. This glorious salvation does four things for us.

Delivers us

1. It delivers us from all our enemies. Christ has

come to overcome everything that is against us. Never does He want us to be crushed or defeated. Always He causes us to triumph if we will but trust and allow Him. How beautifully does the prophet Zechariah illustrate the words of his New Testament namesake, as in his first chapter he gives us his vision of the four horns. Horns that were lifted up against Judah and Jerusalem, representing the evils that are opposed to us from all sides, so that whichever direction we look, north, south, east or west, we sometimes can see nothing but enemies. But he saw four carpenters following the four horns, and as he asked the meaning of this vision he was told that these were come to fray the horns, that is, to soften them, to peel them down, to take their sharpness from them, to render them harmless.

How wondrously does God do this for His people! How He takes the point out of the devil's sting and the enemy's sword-thrust and quenches all the fiery darts of the wicked one with the shield of faith, so that things that seemed sufficient to destroy us pass away harmlessly, and we wonder in great amazement at the providential goodness of our wonderful God. Each of us has often had enough perils to wreck our life and work many a time, but as we look behind we cannot even trace a shadow of the clouds that once covered all our sky. Everything that seemed against us has become a voice in the chorus, "We know that in all things God works for the good of those who love Him" (Romans 8:28a).

Delivered to serve

2. We are delivered from our enemies that we "might serve him without fear" (Luke 1:74). Our fears are sometimes worse than our enemies. Who of us is there that has not spent hours and days fighting clouds that never came to rain or lightning? They seemed intensely real, and they hurt as much as if they were real. Christ comes to deliver us from all our fears. He tells us that the king of fear is the devil, and that fear from him must always be recognized. As long as we abide in Christ, it is a voice from Satan. If it is a voice from Satan, it is a lie; therefore it is not to be allowed to come into the soul. Indeed, we may turn it into a benediction, and say to Satan as he holds up the shadow, "Thank you very much, for now I know that the opposite is coming—a blessing as glorious as the shadow had been dark." This is the way to get the victory over your fears. Refuse them and extract good out of them, even as the woman of Canaan did from her Savior's refusal and from the dark and discouraging prospect that for a time seemed to overshadow all her cares.

God cannot use you fully in His service if you are loaded down with a pack of worries. You must be rested workers. You must come to Him for rest and then take His yoke upon you.

3. We are delivered that we might serve "in holiness and righteousness before him" (Luke 1:75). You will observe that it is not righteousness and holiness, but holiness first. We often begin the

wrong way and try to get our lives right before our hearts are pure. Like Elisha, let us go up to the spring and put salt there and not in the channels of the river below. Cleanse the fountain and the waters will always be pure. Get the holiness of Christ in your heart, and your life will be regulated with the full tides of life and love. Divine life regulates itself and the more it overflows, the more it purifies.

4. We will serve all the days of our life. We used to think that holiness and victory were for our last days and that if we got too near to God we were being prepared to die and might go soon; indeed, that it was not very safe to be too devout. But thank God, we have found that holiness is to live by and that we need it for earth's duties and trials much more even than for heavenly enjoyments. Christ sanctifies us to "serve him without fear/ in holiness and righteousness before him all our days" (74b–75). We can spring into the very fullness of His grace from the very morning of our conversion. We can go from Egypt to Canaan in less than three months and need not spend 40 years wandering in the wilderness of sin. "Oh, if I only had known of this 25 years ago, how sweetly I could have lived," said the dying Payson as he stood in the last moments of his life looking into heaven, realizing the full salvation that he might have known all his days. Beloved, will we take Him for all the days, and go forth singing?

I'm so glad I've learned to trust Him,

Precious Jesus, Saviour, Friend;
And I know that Thou art with me,
Wilt be with me to the end.

There are two closing thoughts suggested by this figure, on which we will dwell for a moment. In the blessing of Joseph in Deuteronomy 33 it is said that his horns will be like the horn of the unicorn. The unicorn has only one horn, and the idea suggested by the strong figure is that they alone are strong who have no strength but God. The glory of my strength is to have God alone. God is never the fullness of power to us until He alone is our power, until we can say, "Whom have I in heaven but you?/ And earth has nothing I desire besides you" (Psalm 73:25).

The other reference is in connection with the sublime vision of the Lamb in the fifth chapter of Revelation, where we behold Him standing in the midst of the throne having seven horns and seven eyes, representing the seven-fold power and authority with which He is invested, and the seven-fold wisdom of the Holy Ghost which He administers. It is because He suffered and redeemed us that God has invested Him, not only with His own eternal deity and power, but with all the resources of the Father's own fullness, so that He could say as He ascended from earth to heaven, "All authority in heaven and on earth has been given to me" (Matthew 28:18). And yet that power is in the hands of One whom John describes as a "little Lamb." Oh, the ineffable gentleness and nearness combined with majesty and power expressed by this figure. With a hand as soft as a child's, a touch as gentle as a mother's, and yet a scepter as mighty as omnipotence, He sits on the heavenly throne, so near and yet so great, so tender and yet so mighty, the blended gentleness and almightiness of the Lamb that is in the midst of the throne.

He is our Horn of Salvation. He has visited us and redeemed us, and He must reign until all our enemies will be made His footstool. Let us join in the chorus that swells in this chapter in billows and billows of praise, surging and surging out to the confines of the universe until "every creature in heaven and on earth and under the earth and on the sea, and all that is in them, [is] singing:

> To him who sits on the throne and to the
>   Lamb
> be praise and honor and glory and power,
>   for ever and ever! (Revelation 5:13)

The Key of David

To the angel of the church in Philadelphia write:

These are the words of him who is holy and true, who holds the key of David. What he opens no one can shut, and what he shuts no one can open. (Revelation 3:7)

The seven epistles to the churches in Revelation contain the last message of Christ to the Church today. It would seem natural to suppose that the seven churches He chose to receive these final messages were in some respect representative of the whole Church to the end of time. They are singularly descriptive of the epochs that have passed over the Church since the days of John.

The first, the church in Ephesus, perfectly represents the church of the days of John, strong in works, but beginning to decline in love. The next, Smyrna, is true to the life of the next age of Christianity, the age of persecution. The third, the church in Pergamos, has some strong resemblance to the worldly church of the days of Constantine and succeeding emperors. The church in Thyatira is almost a perfect type of the apostasy which followed through the rise of the Papacy, with that woman Jezebel on the throne and the depths of Satan beneath her seat of ecclesiastical pride and wickedness.

Then comes the church in Sardis. "You have a reputation of being alive, but are dead" (3:1b). This is a sure and perfect type of the middle ages and the absolute death of spiritual life, with the exception of a few names, even in Sardis, "who have not soiled their clothes" (4a).

Then there is a sudden burst of light—the church of Philadelphia. This message is all promise, encouragement and love. It is the dawn of Reformation. It is the gathering out of the little flock before the end. They have kept His word; they have not denied His name. They will be kept through the hour of temptation and tribulation. They will be established as pillars in the temple of God. They will be enrolled in the New Jerusalem. They will be received into the intimacy of Jesus. They will have an open door which none can shut.

There is one more picture, the church of the Laodiceans, strong, proud, wealthy, self-sufficient, lukewarm and about to be rejected. This is the second apostasy. It is apostate Protestantism. It is the worldly church, which already in our day is beginning to show signs of this final portrait; and with it comes the Master's hand upon the door, and the solemn warning, "I stand at the door and knock" (20). The end is just about to come. But in the previous picture the end is also about to come, and the solemn message even there is, "I am coming soon. Hold on to what you have, so that no one will take your crown" (11), so that these two pictures of Philadelphia and Laodicea both belong to the end. The one is the picture of the little flock of simple faithful ones; the other is the picture of the great worldly church contemporary with Philadelphia and about to be rejected by the Lord at His coming.

It is of this sixth picture of the little Philadelphian church that we wish to consider, or rather of the Master in the attitude in which He addresses to them His cheering message. There are three great and blessed names.

He that is holy

He is holy; therefore, He expects us to be holy for His message is, "Be holy, because I am holy" (1 Peter 1:16b). He is our example, our standard, and we can never rest behind His footsteps.

He is holy; therefore, He enables us to be holy. His holiness is the source of ours, as well as the sanction and the ground of obligation, for He gives us His own holiness. He enters our heart, becomes our life and lives in us His own pure, heavenly life. Therefore the apostle has said,

Both the one who makes men holy and those who are made holy are of the same family. So

Jesus is not ashamed to call them brothers. (Hebrews 2:11)

Jesus said in His own parting prayer, "For them I sanctify myself, that they too may be truly sanctified" (John 17:19).

This did not mean that Christ required to be made holy, as if He were unholy, but He devoted Himself in the sense of entire consecration to this one thing, the sanctification of His people. He set Himself apart for our sakes that we might be truly sanctified, and as we receive Him to dwell within us we receive the sanctification. We receive the Holy One and He becomes our holiness, and "who has become . . . our righteousness, holiness and redemption" (1 Corinthians 1:30). This is the secret of our holiness, to receive Him that is holy, to abide in Him that is holy and to let Him live in us His own heavenly life.

He that is true

This is the picture of the Faithful Promiser. It means His words are true. "Does he speak and then not act?/ Does he promise and not fulfill?" (Numbers 23:19b). How many precious words of promise has He spoken! How many things has He spoken to us! How many has He to speak to us today! Earth and heaven will pass away, but one jot or one tittle of His promises shall in no wise pass away, until all are fulfilled. Every one of them has come to us with the mighty preface, "These are the words of him who is holy and true" (Revelation 3:7a). Let

us rest in them, let us wait for them, for though
they tarry, they will surely come, and they will not
tarry long. He Himself has endorsed them and is
their personal Guarantee.

On an old mosque in Syria there is a strange and
beautiful illustration of God's eternal and un-
changing word. It was a Christian church and it
had on its front, worked in the stone, the words of
God, "Thy kingdom is an everlasting kingdom, and
thy truth endureth to all generations" (Psalm
145:13, KJV).

When the Moslems conquered Palestine they
captured the old church, plastered over the front
and wrote another inscription in honor of the false
prophet in blazing and resplendent letters of gold.
But as the centuries have gone by, the plaster has
fallen off. The transient record of human sin and
pride has perished, and the deeply written record
of God's Word stands out bold and clear, as a
solemn intimation that all men's works and words
shall pass away, but the Word of our God shall
stand forever.

But it means much more than this. Back of all is
His own true heart. He Himself is true, our faithful, unchangeable Friend, and the Guarantee of the
certainty and stability of everything that we value
and hold in Him. God is much more to the
Christian's faith than even His Word. Abraham
believed God, and therefore he believed His Word.
It is because we can trust Him that we can trust
His promises. How we value a true heart! How we
rest in a faithful friend! How we love to lean on one

that we know is loyal to the core! Christ is absolutely true. He loved us from the beginning; He will love us to the end. It is because He chose us knowing all, anticipating all, prepared for the worst, that His love is everlasting. He is so true that He will keep us true. Think of some of the assurances of His faithfulness. He has said,

> Never will I leave you;
>   never will I forsake you. (Hebrews 13:5b)

> He will keep you strong to the end, so that you will be blameless on the day of our Lord Jesus Christ. God, who has called you into fellowship with his Son Jesus Christ our Lord, is faithful. (1 Corinthians 1:8–9)

> And God is faithful; he will not let you be tempted beyond what you can bear. But when you are tempted, he will also provide a way out so that you can stand up under it. (1 Corinthians 10:13)

> So then, those who suffer according to God's will should commit themselves to their faithful Creator and continue to do good. (1 Peter 4:19)

> May God himself, the God of peace, sanctify you through and through. May your whole spirit, soul and body be kept blameless at the coming of our Lord Jesus Christ. The one who

calls you is faithful and he will do it. (1 Thessalonians 5:23–24)

So then we have the faithfulness of God vouched for our sanctification, for our preservation, for our deliverance, for our temptation, for our comfort and support in trial and suffering, for all we can trust Him up to the coming of our Lord Jesus Christ. And we can trust Him with all our heart, with all our weight, giving all our cares to Him because He cares for us, trusting in the Lord Jehovah forever, for He is the Rock of Ages.

But still further, "He that is true" is the Guarantee of our true-heartedness and stability. He will keep us true. We can take Him for our steadfastness.

Not only is God at the heaven-side to anchor the cable there; but He is also heart-side, through the Holy Ghost, to fasten it here, so that it will not slip as it holds us.

And so this precious epistle is full of promises of keeping. While on the one side it bids us hold fast that which we have, that no man take our crown, on the other it promises, "I will also keep you from the hour of trial that is going to come upon the whole world to test those who live on the earth" (Revelation 3:10), and still more strongly, "Him who overcomes I will make a pillar in the temple of my God. Never again will he leave it" (12).

Thank God we can take Him for our courage, for our steadfastness, for He "is able to keep you from falling and to present you before his glorious presence without fault and with great joy" (Jude 24). Blessed is He that is holy, He that is true.

He that has the key of David

This, of course, is a description of Christ as a King, as the real successor to David, King of Israel, the Sovereign Lord of Nature, Providence, the Church, and the Millennial World, the One that controls all destinies and possesses all power and dominion in heaven and in earth. But more particularly, He is the Holder of the key of David, "What he opens no one can shut, and what he shuts no one can open" (Revelation 3:7b).

How many things He opens, and opens forever to His people! He opens the gates of life; for, "I am the gate; whoever enters through me will be saved. He will come in and go out, and find pasture" (John 10:9). He opens the gate of heaven; for into that city shall those only enter that are written in the Lamb's book of life, and over the gate are written the words, "Blessed are those who wash their robes, that they may have the right to the tree of life and may go through the gates into the city" (Revelation 22:14). He opens our heart for His incoming. He won our stubborn will and taught us to trust and love Him and yield ourselves to Him, and He alone can rule and subdue us with His scepter of perfect love.

He opens our eyes to understand His will, and He opens His Word to our understanding, so that we may behold wondrous things out of His law and possess all the treasures of His glorious truth. He opens for us the gates of difficulty and breaks in pieces the gates of brass and cuts in sunder the bars of iron and enables us to go forward through what seem impassible barriers in His work and will. He holds the key of knowledge and opens to us every problem that perplexes and every question that baffles and will be our wisdom and guide in every trying hour.

He opens our way of service, our door of usefulness and prepares us for them, for our work, and our field, and He says to us, "See, I have placed before you an open door that no one can shut." He prepared Paul's work and gave it to him, and He will give you yours if you are ready to do it, and none can hinder, for when He gives it, everything must go away.

He holds the key of human hearts and can open them to your message. He can convict the conscience, influence the will, persuade the heart, draw the sinner to His feet and constrain the reluctant to be willing in the days of His power. He holds the key to every safe and pocketbook, and He can say to you, "I will give you the treasures of darkness,/ riches stored in secret places" (Isaiah 45:3a), and He will provide the means that you need for every undertaking on which He sends you.

He holds the key of providence and can control all events and circumstances in your eternal life, to cooperate with you or become tributary to you in your service for Him. He that opened the prison gates for Peter and rent the bars of the Philippian jail is still the same. He who gave Esther and

Daniel favor in the courts of Persia and Babylon, and made Joseph to be beloved of all he met in the land of Egypt, and gave Paul the friendship of the captain of the guard, and made Cyrus, in the flush of his pride, send forth the captives of Israel to their land, can still open every door and control every heart. "The king's heart is in the hand of the LORD;/ he directs it like a watercourse wherever he pleases" (Proverbs 21:1). He will open for you the pathway of His will, the way in which He would have you go. "I will lead the blind," He says,

> by ways they have not known,
>   along unfamiliar paths I will guide them;
> I will turn the darkness into light before
>   them
>   and make the rough places smooth.
> These are the things I will do;
>   I will not forsake them. (Isaiah 42:16)

> I have raised him up in righteousness, and I will direct all his ways. (Isaiah 45:13, KJV)

> When I act, who can reverse it? (Isaiah 43:13b)

His people's path may lead through Red Seas and Jordans of swollen tides, and Jerichos of formidable and definite power, and Euroclydian's wild tempestuous fire; but He who has already burst through the gates of death and hell will fulfill all His counsel and accomplish all His perfect will.

When He makes bare His arm,
　Who shall His power withstand,
When He His people's cause maintains,
　Who, who shall stay His hand?

Beloved, will you use your key more faithfully, more trustfully, more constantly? Will you prove more fully than ever that you have One with you who "opens" and no one can shut?

What He shuts

How many things He shuts! He has shut for us the gates of hell, blessed be His name forever. "Therefore, there is now no condemnation for those who are in Christ Jesus" (Romans 8:1), and they will not come into judgment but have passed out of death into life. He holds the keys of death, and its darts cannot touch His children until He permits them. He holds back the gates of temptation. Satan cannot touch one of His children even with a tormenting thought until the Master permits.

There is an "if need be" in our manifold temptations. We are led out of the Spirit into the wilderness to be tempted of the devil. Between every dragon wing or hellish dart and us is the presence of the Holy Ghost, the bosom of Jesus and the shield of faith, and He that was begotten of God keeps us and that wicked one cannot touch us. And therefore He says in this verse, "Since you have kept my command to endure patiently, I will also keep you from the hour of trial that is going to come upon the whole world to test those who live on the earth" (Revelation 3:10). This probably means the last and terrible tribulation from which the saints of God will be taken out and preserved; but it also means many other hours of temptation from which His people are free. One of the terrible calamities of the wicked is that they are tempted above that which they are able to bear; but one of the most blessed promises to a saint is that he will not be so tempted, but that he will be guarded, and when the pressure would be too strong it will be held back.

He also keeps back the floods of sorrow and calamity. In the seventh chapter of Revelation we behold an angel standing in the sky and holding back the winds, lest they should blow upon the earth before the saints of God were sealed. And so God shuts the doors of the natural world, the floodgates of the tides of all evil, and says, "This far you may come and no farther" (Job 38:11), and there the waves are stopped. Fear not, He will deliver you in trial. The floods may have lifted up their voice and made a mighty noise of many waters and the great sea billows. The Lord sitteth King above the floods; yea, the Lord sitteth King forever.

There is another door that He shuts, and that is the door of the inner chamber, where He hides us with Himself, where He takes us into His fellowship, where He gives us His eternal covenant and seals and secures to us "what [we] have entrusted to him for that day" (2 Timothy 1:12b).

In this closing verse He says, "Him who overcomes I will make a pillar in the temple of my God
. . . and the name of the city of my God, the new
Jerusalem, which is coming down out of heaven
from my God; and I will also write on him my new
name" (Revelation 3:12). When God put Noah in
the ark He shut him in. When He takes us into His
bosom He shuts us in. When He gives us His
promises He guarantees them, seals them and
keeps them for us.

The ideas underlying these beautiful figures are
stability, security and intimacy. He will keep us. He
will make us a part of Himself, which is the meaning of the name of God. He will make us part of the
New Jerusalem, giving us a place in His millennial
glory and writing the very name of that city upon
us as if we inseparately belonged to it. And He will
give us the pledge of His own personal and pure intimacy, writing upon us His own new name. This
refers back to the white stone and the name written upon it, which no man could read except he to
whom it was given. This is the token of the secret
love, the special covenant, the confidential
friendship, the inmost, uttermost love of Jesus.

Now unto Him "who is holy and true, who holds
the key of David. What he opens no one can shut,
and what he shuts no one can open" (7) be glory
forever. And He answers back to us, "See, I have
placed before you an open door that no one can
shut" (3:8). It opens up to the glory of His coming
with the crown shining in the light of vision, as He
cries, "I am coming soon. Hold on to what you

have, so that no one will take your crown" (11). And we take Him to hold us, and to hold for us our crown, and then to let us lay it at His blessed feet forever and say, "You who are holy, you who are true, you who have given all and kept all, you will have all the glory forever. Amen."

The Cornerstone

*From Judah will come the cornerstone,/
from him the tent peg [nail, KJV],/ from
him the battle bow,/ from him every
ruler. (Zechariah 10:4)*

The reference of this verse is to the tribe of
Judah, out of which was to come the
cornerstone, the nail and the battle bow. This may
have referred, in the first instance, to earthly kings
and defenders; but, undoubtedly, their ultimate
typical application was to the Lord Jesus Christ,
and to Him indeed the same figures are elsewhere
applied so explicitly as to leave no doubt as to the
scriptural validity of this interpretation.

This metaphor is directly applied to the Lord
Jesus Christ by the Apostle Peter in the second
chapter of his first epistle, verses 4–7,

> As you come to him, the living Stone—
> rejected by men but chosen by God and pre-
> cious to him—you also, like living stones, are

being built into a spiritual house to be a holy priesthood, offering spiritual sacrifices acceptable to God through Jesus Christ. For in Scripture it says:

> "See, I lay a stone in Zion,
>   a chosen and precious cornerstone,
> and the one who trusts in him
>   will never be put to shame."

Now to you who believe, this stone is precious. But to those who do not believe,

> "The stone the builders rejected
>   has become the capstone."

1. The cornerstone is the foundation of the building. It rests upon it. So Christ is our foundation. There we rest our hopes for eternity and for everything. "For no one can lay any foundation other than the one already laid, which is Jesus Christ" (1 Corinthians 3:11).

2. The cornerstone regulates the entire building. From the cornerstone all other locations and measurements are taken. So Christ gives direction to all our life. Everything should be shaped with reference to Him as the center. We can build no broader than the foundation and cornerstone, and the walls must be ever vertical to it or they will fall.

Our whole Christian life must be under the absolute control of the Lord Jesus, and both in its lateral and vertical lines, as it reaches toward others and touches heaven, it must be according to His mind and will, His Spirit and holy example.

3. The cornerstone unites the building. Without it there can be only one wall, and a wall is not a building. It is in Jesus that we touch each other and become united in our Christian life and in our inmost spirit. A common creed will never unite us; a common work will not permanently unite us; only a common life will. The true secret of unity in the universal Christian Church is to live closer to Jesus. A deep spiritual life will always sweep away the consciousness, at least, of sectarian barriers. If we would love each other and be closely united, let us be filled with His love, and pressing hard to His bosom we will touch each other in the sweetest fellowship of Christian life.

4. The cornerstone bears the record of the building. The name is on the stone, and so we should bear the name of Jesus, and no name be seen but His. The date is there, and, although the stone was laid long before the finishing of the building, yet the edifice always bears the date of the stone.

So the true date of our salvation is Calvary and the resurrection. It was then that we died with Him; it was then that we rose with Him; it was then that our salvation, our healing, our redemption was finished; and we simply receive the completed work of Christ.

And so the story of the building is written upon His hands, His feet and His heart, and the eternal recompenses will be given according to the inscriptions that He holds.

5. The cornerstone is the ornamental stone of the building. It is often made of polished granite or marble, or still more precious material, and it is the object of observation and the ornament of the structure. So Jesus bears the glory. Unto you, therefore, who believe, He is precious, or literally, is for an ornament. We are not to bear the praise or the glory, or to decorate ourselves with the insignia of human grandeur, but to be hidden upon His bosom and to hold Him up before the world as our honor and our praise, ever crying, "To him who sits on the throne and/ to the Lamb/ be praise and honor and glory and/ power/ for ever and ever!" (Revelation 5:13b)

> Not I, but Christ, be honored, praised, exalted;
> Not I, but Christ, be seen, be known, be heard.
> Not I, but Christ, in every look and motion;
> Not I, but Christ, in every thought and word.
>
> Oh, to be saved from myself, dear Lord,
> Oh, to be lost in Thee;
> Oh, that it might be no more I,
> But Christ that lives in me.

The nail

In the 22nd chapter of Isaiah this figure is more fully referred to:

> The key to the house of David; what he opens no one can shut, and what he shuts no one can open. I will drive him like a peg into a

firm place; he will be a seat of honor for the house of his father. All the glory of his family will hang on him: its offspring and off-shoots—all its lesser vessels, from the bowls to all the jars. (22–24)

In the third chapter of Revelation this passage is quoted by the Lord Jesus with respect to Himself: "These are the words of him who is holy and true, who holds the key of David. What he opens no one can shut, and what he shuts no one can open" (7).

The passage here refers directly to Christ, and it is in this passage that He is called the "nail fastened in the sure place" (Isaiah 22:23, KJV), on which is to be hung all the glory of the Father's house.

There are two special uses of a nail. The first is to secure and fasten, and so Christ is the security of our hopes and lives. He keeps us by His intercession, by His life, by our union with Himself. Second, a nail is to hang things upon, and this is the special sense in which it is here used. The Father has hung everything upon Jesus. All the glory of the Father's house is upon Him. "All things have been committed to me by my Father" (Luke 10:22a), He says. "The Father loves the Son and has placed everything into his hands" (John 3:35). There is no attribute of power, wisdom or love in God which Jesus does not fully possess, and has not the right to communicate to us to use for our well-being. But not only has the Father hung everything upon Him, but He can hang all our graces upon Him. We are not to hang them upon ourselves. We do not and never will possess anything of ourselves. It is not that we are to add our virtues to our own person, but we are to take Christ to be in our hearts "as a nail fastened in the sure place" and then upon Him we may hang the faith, the love, the peace, the gentleness, the patience, and all the graces of spirit, until our heart becomes a wardrobe with a thousand dresses ready for use as we need them in each new situation and act of life.

The figure represents the nail as bearing upon it, not only all the glory of the Father's house, but the offspring and the issue, and all vessels, both the bowls and jars. The offspring and issue have reference, perhaps, to our being born of Him as His very offspring and issue and fastened to Him by ties of blood and life. Or it may refer to our offspring and issue, our spiritual fruit, all of which we must receive through Him, for our power is not our own, but is hung upon Christ, and all our work must be handed over to Him and kept by Him as the nail on which we leave every precious thing.

The bowls and jars hung upon this nail have reference to the various needs of life, all of which are supplied from Him. On this blessed nail are hanging cups of every size, which we can fill, and from which we can drink whenever we are thirsty, and there is no want so small but we can find it met in His name and life and love. The jars, or vessels of wine, refer to the deeper joys, blessings of our communion with Him. As there is no cup too small for Him to fill, so there is no need too deep, no joy too divine for Him to satisfy.

The certainty and security

The sure place in which this nail is fastened has reference to the certainty and security of the blessing which we have in Christ. All else is liable to fail, but that which we hang upon Him will stand forever. The confidences we repose in others and ourselves are fragile, but this only can never be removed. This hope is an anchor of the soul, both sure and steadfast.

First, this nail has been fastened into the cross of Calvary, where our salvation was completed. Second, this nail has been fastened into the throne in the ascension and resurrection of Christ, guaranteeing our complete salvation. Third, it may be fastened in our hearts as the very essence and substance of our inmost life, a life so certain, a keeping so infinite and divine, that we can say, "I know whom I have believed, and am convinced that he is able to guard what I have entrusted to him for that day" (2 Timothy 1:12b).

There are two ways of fastening a nail. One is to drive a cut nail into the wood and just leave it. The other is to take a wrought nail made of malleable iron and drive it through and a little beyond, and there clinch it. This kind of work never draws, and this is the sort of nail that Christ is when truly taken in the committal of faith.

Christ has clinched the nail on His side. "I give them eternal life, and they shall never perish; no one can snatch them out of my hand" (John 10:28). This is the nail driven; but listen, "My Father, who has given them to me, is greater than all; and no one can snatch them out of my Father's hand" (29). That is the nail clinched.

The battle bow

The first thing suggested by the bow is that Christ is the spring of our lives. If you want a spirit that sweeps the heavens and reaches out into the infinite possiblities of God's boundlessness, take Christ to dwell in your heart.

Next, the figure suggests defense. Christ is our defense against the enemy, but we have to use Him as you would use a bow. A bow lying on the ground is of no use. A bow unstrung is of no use. You must take it, draw the string, pull the bow and shoot the arrows and your enemies will fall with every shaft.

Again, the bow suggests an arrow. The bow is useless without an arrow. The arrows are God's promises and our prayers, pointed by definite desires, directed by the will of God, winged by faith and holy expectation and then sent forth with the strong hand and the full momentum of the faith of God to reach the heavens and the uttermost parts of our needs and our difficulties.

We have a beautiful example of these arrows in the 13th chapter of Second Kings. The great prophet of Israel was dying, and Joash, his grateful king, came to visit him, and cried, as he knelt beside him, "My father! My father! The chariots and horsemen of Israel!" (14b). Then Elisha proceeded to give the king some expression and evidence of his real help, stronger than mere words. He bade him take a bow and arrows that were lying by his side, and, putting his hands alongside the king's, he commanded him to pull the string to its utmost tension and shoot an arrow. As it sped away into the fields beyond, he cried, "The LORD's arrow of victory, the arrow of victory over Aram! . . . You will completely destroy the Arameans in Aphek" (17b). But this was not enough. He must take up the arrows and prove for himself the strength and completeness of his faith, and so the prophet bids him strike the ground. He does it three times and then stops. The old prophet looks grave and angry. "You should have struck the ground five or six times; then you would have defeated Aram and completely destroyed it. But now you will defeat it only three times" (19b). He had only taken half a blessing, and that was all that he would have.

As we take the bow of faith, there is another hand that holds and guides it. Let us not fear to pull the string to its utmost tension, for this bow will never break. Christ is the battle bow, and His hand is pulling the string with ours, and we can have all we dare to claim. Let the arrow be very definite, and then let us not stay until we have covered the whole circle of possible need and blessing. He will be only too glad to give us all we dare to claim and grieved only because we take so little. May the Lord help us to know

. . . his incomparably great power for us who

believe. That power is like the working of his mighty strength, which he exerted in Christ when he raised him from the dead and seated him at his right hand in the heavenly realms, far above all rule and authority, power and dominion, and every title that can be given, not only in the present age but also in the one to come. (Ephesians 1:19–21)

The Refiner

But who can endure the day of his coming? Who can stand when he appears? For he will be like a refiner's fire or a launderer's soap. He will sit as a refiner and purifier of silver; he will purify the Levites and refine them like gold and silver. Then the LORD will have men who will bring offerings in righteousness. (Malachi 3:2–3)

This is the last Old Testament prophetic message respecting the coming Messiah. The first verse tells of two messengers who are soon to appear: one is the forerunner, the other the Savior, the great angel of the covenant who appeared to Abraham and Moses and who in the Old Testament ages was the manifestation of Jehovah to His people.

The special reference is to His purifying work. He is to be distinguished from all former teachers and messengers by His sin-cleansing power. He is to

"sit as a refiner and purifier of silver," and to
"purify the Levites . . . who will bring offerings in
righteousness." Other messengers could bring
reformation; He is to bring regeneration. Others
were reprovers of sin; but He brings the power that
takes the sin away.

Malachi's message was echoed four centuries
later by John the Baptist as he stood among the
thousands who came to him for deliverance from
their sins, and he felt his helplessness to grant
them what they needed and longed for a stronger
and diviner hand to cleanse and keep. "I baptize
you with water for repentance" (Matthew 3:11a),
but while he said it he knew that the men who
came to him to confess their sins would soon be
again immersed in sin and powerless to overcome
it, and he longed intensely for one who could not
only reprove and forgive, but who could renew and
radically cleanse the heart from intrinsic evil. And
so he added: "But after me will come one who is
more powerful than I, whose sandals I am not fit to
carry. He will baptize you with the Holy Spirit and
with fire" (11b).

This was indeed the meaning of the glorious
name given to the Savior before He came, "Jesus,
because he will save his people from their sins"
(1:21b), and this is one of the radical distinctions
between the Old Testament and the New. The latter provides for a complete and perfect cleansing
and purification of our entire being from the
power of evil, such as the law could never bring.

Let us inquire for a little what are the essential

differences between the Old and the New Testaments, the law and the gospel in the provision they make for our spiritual cleansing.

A higher standard

First, Christ brings us a far higher standard, no less indeed than a divine example. His command to us is, "Be holy, because I am holy" (1 Peter 1:16b). "Be perfect therefore, as your heavenly Father is perfect" (Matthew 5:48). He requires of us not only a lofty human character, but complete resemblance to the divine image. "Love one another. As I have loved you . . . " (John 13:34). He has chosen us that we should "be conformed to the likeness of his Son" (Romans 8:29b). "Put on the new self, which is being renewed in knowledge in the image of its Creator" (Colossians 3:9b). He that abides in Him ought to "walk as Jesus did" (1 John 2:6b).

But not only does it unfold a higher standard, but it reveals a deeper, more interior life, a life that reaches even to the heart, the thoughts, the motives, the desires. It requires us to love the Lord with all our heart and soul and mind and strength, to not only abstain from impurity, but from unholy thought and feeling; not only to do right, but to do right from a right motive. The word for purity in the New Testament is singleness of heart. Murder is hatred, adultery is evil desire, and the righteousness of the kingdom a radical and divine renewing of the inmost being and all the principles, motives and aims of life.

Not only so, but the righteousness of the New Testament reaches to all sides of our being and relationships, internal as well as external. The Old Testament had sacred persons, times and things; but under the New Testament everything is sacred. One day in seven was holy to the Lord, but now every day should be a Sabbath in its true spirit. One place was His sanctuary, but now every place should be dedicated to His glory. One class of men was separated to sacred priestly functions; but now we are "a kingdom and priests to serve God" (Revelation 1:6a), and expected to be equally holy and near to Him. One class of duties was holier than another; but now everything we do may be done unto His glory, and pleasing in His sight.

And so the standard of New Testament holiness is higher, deeper and broader than the Old. Therefore, we find some things even in the morality of the former which would not be accepted under the New. Zechariah, the prophet, dying under the hand of Joash, prayed, "May the Lord see this and call you to account" (2 Chronicles 24:22b). Stephen looked up from the blows of his murderers and cried, "Lord, do not hold this sin against them" (Acts 7:60b).

Complete provision

Second, Christ makes complete provision in His atonement for our cleansing. The offerings of the Old Testament were types of this future provision for the cleansing of the offerer; but the Apostle well says in Hebrews, that they were "only a shadow"

(10:1), but Christ has come with His own blood to make full and final provision for our entire cleansing. "It is impossible for the blood of bulls and goats to take away sins" (4). Then said He, " I come to do your will, O God. . . . by that will, we have been made holy through the sacrifice of the body of Jesus Christ once for all. . . . Because by one sacrifice he has made perfect forever those who are being made holy" (9–14). It is therefore true that the atonement of Jesus Christ has provided for our entire cleansing from evil and the sanctification of our entire being to God. If this is so, whatever the difficulties may be, it is our redemption right, and if it be so, it is the redemption right of all believers. It is not an exclusive or exceptional distinction which a few saintly ones may claim, but it is covered by the blood of the cross and the "whosoever" of the gospel. If we are not entering into it as a personal experience, we are to that extent allowing Christ to have died for us in vain and coming short of the full inheritance. Do you realize that it is your privilege, your purchased right, to be holy and that for this purpose your Savior shed His precious blood, and you are stabbing Him with a new wound if you let Him die in vain?

A living source

Third, Christ has not only revealed a higher holiness and purchased for us the right to it; but He has risen again to become for us the living source of that holiness through union with His own person. He has offered to come to us in His person and to become to each of us an indwelling life which will literally reproduce in us His own purity and enable us to live among men even as He lived. This is something which the Old Testament saints never knew. God was *with* Moses and Elijah and the men at Babylon; but God is *in* the humblest of His saints who sincerely receive Him. This is the mystery hid from ages and generations, "Christ in you, the hope of glory" (Colossians 1:27b). This is "God's secret wisdom, a wisdom . . . none of the rulers of this age understood" (1 Corinthians 2:7–8a), Christ who has become for us wisdom from God—that is, our righteousness, holiness and redemption. This is the great provision of the gospel, a living personal Savior, Christ our life. This is our all-sufficiency for every situation and trial and difficulty, "I can do everything through him who gives me strength" (Philippians 4:13). This is the source of holy living and holy usefulness, "If a man remains in me and I in him, he will bear much fruit; apart from me you can do nothing" (John 15:5b). This renders our failure inexcusable. This makes our responsibility for a holy life tenfold greater. Beloved, have we recognized that God is meeting each of us with a full divine provision for a life of holiness and victory and that He holds us responsible, not so much to do it ourselves, as to receive from Him the grace and power that will enable us to do it?

Fourth, the preeminent provision Jesus Christ has made in the gospel for our cleansing is the gift of the Holy Ghost. He sent to us from heaven the third person of the Divine Trinity to take up His abode in our heart, to impart to us the very life of Christ, to teach us, to lead us, to train us in our Christian life and to carry on the whole work of our cleansing and spiritual perfecting until the Refiner can see His image mirrored in the silver, and we are prepared to be jewels in the day of His coming. It is one thing to be cleansed from sin and surely that ought to be true of every Christian, but it is a different thing to be refined by God's holy fire until we have been brought into all the fullness of His will and reflect in all things His holy image. It is this thorough work of the Holy Spirit to which God is calling us in these words, where He sits as "a refiner and purifier of silver," calmly working and waiting until His purpose is fulfilled.

The Holy Bride

In the picture given of the Holy Bride as she sits waiting for the coming Lord, it is said in the book of Revelation that it was granted to her to be arrayed in fine linen, clean and bright, or lustrous. It is one thing to have the linen clean; it is another to have it bright and lustrous. You may take your linen from the clothes line, and there is no spot on it; but when you take it from the laundry, it is not only spotless, but lustrous, polished, shining with the gloss of skillful hands, as if it be costly embroidery or lace adorned with all the delicate touches of the needle and the loom, arranged in beautiful order and taste. It is one thing for the gold to be cleansed from the dross; it is another for it to be shaped in all the skill of the silversmith's art. It is one thing to have sin burned out; it is quite another to have the glory burned in.

And so we read in Daniel, "Many will be purified, made spotless and refined" (12:10a). The purification is the primary work of sanctification, but the making white is that which John expresses by the word *lustrous*. It is the refining, the adorning, the completing of the work in the minutiae of detail. This is the work which the Holy Spirit is carrying on in all our hearts as fully as we will let Him. Perhaps He has delivered you from sin, but now He is endeavoring to deliver you from self. There is nothing more truly productive of miseries and failures in Christian life than the spirit of self, even in good persons.

Ask yourself where all cares and worries come from, and you will find from some thought of self, from some fear about yourself, from some consideration of your interests, rights, wrongs, grievances or troubles. It will be a haven of rest to you, and a source of great blessing to others, if you will wholly cancel all thoughts of yourself and will truly say that all your acts and prayers are for others and for your Master's cause. The moment you begin to live this life you will enter into perfect peace and you will find that God has taken up your cause.

Perhaps He is refining you from your natural life and lifting you into a spiritual life and love. Your affections are, perhaps, merely human, and they are absorbing others for your own gratification rather than for God's will and glory and are keeping you on a lower plane. God wants them transformed and transfigured into the heavenly love that will be abiding and eternal, the millennial life into which He is leading you already, even before the coming of your Lord. He is crucifying you to your loves and links that they may be reformed in God and so formed that they may be forever.

Have you ever seen a skeletonized bouquet? The leaves in their natural beauty are soft and green, but fading; in a few hours they will wither away, and their beauty will be dead. But after some skillful woman's hands have touched them, they come forth from the bleaching whiter than the driven snow, delicate, ethereal, as flowers of paradise, every fiber of the skeleton standing out in fine and clear relief, and yet so purified from the earthly and fleshly covering that they are more beautiful than before. Their beauty will never wither. They stand in your vase or cabinet the same through the passing years, the substance of that which you once possessed in a lower form. It is a cold and imperfect figure, yet it expresses something of the refining process through which God is putting our hearts and transforming our earthly loves into heavenly ties that will last forever, not like those dry, skeletonized leaves, but with a deeper love than they had before, a love more calm, more pure, more peaceful, more unselfish, more divine.

The higher grace of love

Perhaps He is teaching you the higher grace of

love and leading you through the 13th chapter of First Corinthians. Some of you know how slowly you get through it. Perhaps you have the longsuffering and kindness, the humility and modesty of the fourth verse. Perhaps you have the unselfishness of the fifth verse, but have you progressed to the "not easily angered" (5), to the "does not delight in evil" (6)? Perhaps you can "always protect" in the seventh verse with a grin-and-bear-it stoicism, but have you reached the next clause, "always trusts, always hopes"? Do you have the spirit that so refuses to believe evil that there is really nothing to bear, that cuts the sinews of your troubles by ignoring them and refusing to believe them, and by looking at the people that have wronged you with such a loving trustfulness that you will not believe evil of them even if it seems to be true, and if you cannot quite believe that it is not so, you will, like your heavenly Father, say, "It should not be, and I will think of them as if it were not true"?

For my own sake I always try to refuse to believe it if I can, and if I cannot believe good of people at the present, it is an infinite comfort to me to ask the Lord to make it true. Then I believe that He will make it true, and hope for them with that confidence which enables me to count the things which are not as if they were, and henceforth think of the erring one in the light of my hope, in the light of their own future, as though already in heaven and the perfection and glory of the Father's life.

Beloved, that erring brother some day will be brighter than the sun, and you will love him without a recollection of your present grievances against him. Think of this now as if it were so and so anticipate the future and so rise out of the present that you will act under the influence of that which shall be, and you can so labor and pray to make it real.

What about the eighth verse, "Love never fails"? You have a great deal of love, and uniformly triumph, but once in a while you sort of claim the privilege of a temporary failure. You do not think it very wrong if you occasionally break down, and so your weak link destroys the entire chain. God is leading you through this to that victory which never fails, so that love which goes forth exclaiming, "But thanks be to God, who always leads us in triumphal procession in Christ and through us spreads everywhere the fragrance of the knowledge of him" (2 Corinthians 2:14).

The Refiner may be taking you through the experience of patience and strengthening you with all might according to His glorious power unto all patience and longsuffering with joyfulness. Perhaps you have the patience and the longsuffering, but do you have the joyfulness? And so we might take all the lessons, and trace His gentle leading and teaching through the discipline of our spiritual life as He is bringing us closer and closer to His own glorious likeness.

A jeweler once told a lady that he kept the silver in the fire until he could see his face in it; and so the great Refiner sits down quietly, slowly, at the crucible where our hearts are consuming, and waits until He can see His image in our hearts and souls. Then He dismisses the firemen, carries away the ashes, stops the flames and takes the silver and pours it into the mold of something lovely and heavenly, where it becomes a vessel for His grace and love, or perhaps as jars to carry His wine and water to His perishing, suffering children, for He is refining and purifying us as silver is tried.

The service of sanctified men and women is immeasurably more precious to God in its most trivial forms than all we can do or give when our hearts are swept by earthly passion or influenced by selfish or unholy motives.

CHAPTER
14

The Baptizer

I would not have known him, except that the one who sent me to baptize with water told me, "The man on whom you see the Spirit come down and remain is he who will baptize with the Holy Spirit." (John 1:33)

This is one of the names given to our dear Lord. It is especially becoming that we should greatly honor the Holy Spirit because He never honors Himself, but ever holds up the person of Jesus Christ, and hides behind the glory of Him whom He loves to reveal. It is not, however, of the Holy Spirit directly that this passage speaks, but of Him who sends the Holy Spirit "He who will baptize with the Holy Spirit," our blessed Lord, to whom we owe this most precious gift of the New Testament dispensation.

In what sense does Christ baptize with the Holy Spirit?

The Spirit is His gift as He is the Father's gift.

166

The greatest gift of the New Testament was Jesus; the greatest gift of Jesus was the Spirit; and the Spirit brings both the Father and the Son into our hearts and lives.

He removed the hindrances

1. Jesus is the giver of the Holy Spirit inasmuch as He has removed the hindrances to the coming of the Spirit into our hearts. The great hindrance was sin. The Holy Spirit is just the presence of God, and God cannot dwell in an unholy temple any more than Noah's dove could rest upon the earth while the floods of judgment and the carcasses of corrupt flesh covered the earth. Not until the flood had passed and all flesh had died, and the earth had been cleansed by its great baptism of judgment could the dove rest, not merely for a moment upon the boughs of the olive trees, but all over the land, to fly abroad and build its nest and rear its broods wherever it could find a sheltering branch.

So the Holy Spirit, under the Old Testament, could not rest in the hearts of men. Often He visited them, even as the dove went forth from the ark. Often He revealed the olive branch of peace and covenant. Often He came to the hearts of men with divine light, life and help; but the human breast was not His home until after Jesus had finished His work of atonement. But when, through the cross of Calvary, the judgment of sin was accomplished, and, in the death of the Substitute, sinful man was recognized as dead to the flesh, as judged, as crucified, then He went forth to rest and reside on earth and to make the hearts of men His home.

Just as soon as it was demonstrated by the ascension of Jesus that sin was judged and God was satisfied for guilty man, immediately the Holy Spirit came down from heaven. And so in the individual life, just as soon as sin is confessed and judged and the blood of the great sacrifice is appropriated and Jesus Christ accepted as the propitiation and the cleansing of the heart, the blessed Comforter loves to come into the holy temple of our inmost being to dwell as our Guest, our Friend, our Guide, our Master, the Representative to us of God and the Executive in us and for us of His holy will. To Jesus we owe all this. But for His redeeming work, the blessed presence of God could never come to dwell within us; but now the message has gone forth to every sinful soul, "Repent and be baptized, . . . in the name of Jesus Christ so that your sins may be forgiven. And you will receive the gift of the Holy Spirit" (Acts 2:38).

Have you accepted the great atonement? Have you received the cleansing blood? Have you been reconciled and sanctified, and has the way been opened by the precious blood of the great High Priest into the Holy of Holies of your inmost being, for the Shekinah of His glory to shine within and reveal the light of the knowledge of the glory of God in the face of Jesus? Is there any cloud of sin hiding and hindering that divine indwelling? He is able to clear it all away. Come to His blessed feet, come to His sprinkled blood, come to His throne of grace, come to the great Sacrifice, come to the cross of Calvary, come to the great High Priest, come to Jesus, and He will cleanse you by His blood and baptize you with His Holy Spirit.

Received into His own person

2. Jesus baptizes with the Holy Spirit inasmuch as He received the Holy Spirit into His own person, and for three and a half years walked through Galilean Judea *"in the Spirit,"* which He now gives to us. He received the third person of the Godhead into personal union with Himself so that He could send Him forth, not as another Spirit, but as His own Spirit. This is very precious and truly wonderful. The Holy Spirit is not to us now what He was under the Old Testament, purely the Spirit of Deity, but He is, if we can understand what it means, the Spirit that dwelt in the human and divine Christ; the Spirit that (if we may say it with reverence) was softened and in some sense humanized by union with Jesus; the Spirit that loved John and Mary, that took the little children to His bosom, that had compassion for the multitude, that wept for Jerusalem, that said to the poor woman, "Go now and leave your life of sin" (John 8:11b), that whispered, "Do not let your hearts be troubled" (John 14:1b), that talked with the woman of Samaria, that forgave and restored Peter, that overlooked all Thomas' unbelief, that bore so patiently the shame of the judgment hall and endured the agony of the cross, that walked

and talked on the way to Emmaus, so simply, and yet with such human tenderness and nearness. And so Jesus received Him and spoke all His words and did all His works through the Spirit; and now He gives to us the very same Spirit that dwelt in Him. In Romans, Paul speaks of the Spirit of Christ, and says, "But if Christ is in you, your body is dead because of sin, yet your spirit is alive because of righteousness" (8:10), and "If anyone does not have the Spirit of Christ, he does not belong to Christ" (9b).

He is waiting today to give you His own very Spirit, to breathe upon you and say, "Receive the Holy Spirit" (20:22b). You may take Him warm from the bosom of Jesus, sweet as the breath of His love, pure as the light of His holiness, mighty as the strength of His omnipotence, and, in some sense, colored and softened by the very humanity of our incarnate Lord.

Directly sent Him

3. Jesus baptizes with the Holy Spirit in the sense that He distinctly sent Him on the day of Pentecost from heaven to earth. It was His promise that He would do so. "Unless I go away, the Counselor [Comforter, KJV] will not come to you; but if I go, I will send him to you" (16:7b). And so Peter, speaking of His coming, says, "He has received from the Father the promised Holy Spirit and has poured out what you now see and hear" (Acts 2:33). This was a distinct and actual transaction which involved the most stupendous issues and

relations. On that day and in that moment a real person, a divine person, actually changed His residence and removed from heaven to earth and has ever since resided, not in heaven, but in this world. With the sound of that mighty rushing wind, a procession as glorious as the ascension of Jesus took place. The Holy Dove, the mighty Paraclete, came down from heaven to return no more until the dispensation of the gospel will have closed. And from that hour His residence has been in this world in the hearts of Christ's people and the sacred sanctuary of His body, the Church.

Let us fully realize this. The Spirit is not now in heaven, and we never need ask Him to come from heaven. He is present, and we have only to receive Him for He has already come. The mighty baptism has been commanded and imparted; and, just as the air is charged with electricity and you have but to absorb it from the atmosphere, just as the atmosphere is saturated with moisture and the cool pitcher has only to absorb the dew, so the Holy Spirit is all around us. The spaces about us are filled with His presence. His ear is within whispering distance of every heart, and we have but to become receiving vessels adjusted to His touch, and He flows in to fill every channel of our being as naturally as the air enters the open lungs, as the light floods the lifted window, as the sun shines wherever there is any object to receive His radiance. Beloved, the Holy Spirit has come; the day of Pentecost is past; the Spirit of God is here. Will you receive Him?

Must come to each heart for itself

4. But there is yet a personal baptism with the Holy Spirit that must come to each heart for itself. To each of us must be applied personally the great atonement, to each of us must come the actual presence of the Comforter, and Jesus is the One that will bring this to pass. It is not the Holy Spirit to whom you are to pray, but it is the Savior. It is He that baptizes with the Holy Spirit.

Go to Jesus for Him, put yourself at His dear feet, take Him as your Savior, take Him as your Sanctifier, trust Him to give you this most precious gift. Claim it and refuse to let Him go without its fullness. Hold fast to His loving feet. Claim your birthright, your redemption right, what He so longs to give you. Obey His voice. Follow His directions. Thank Him for the faintest touch that answers your prayer. Follow on in the light He gives, even in a gleam of radiance, and you will know the Lord in all the fullness of His glory and love and eternally praise Him who baptizes with the Holy Spirit.

What is involved in this great baptism and blessing? It is different from the conversion of the soul and the work of the Spirit in regeneration. That is the birth of the soul; this is the baptism. Just as Jesus Himself was born of the Spirit in Mary's womb but 30 years later was baptized of the Spirit on the banks of the Jordan, so each of us is born of the Spirit in the moment of our conversion. But we are baptized of the Spirit when we yield ourselves fully to Christ, and, like Him on Jordan's banks, enter upon our life-work for God.

It is a direct personal coming of God's Spirit into the heart and a complete possessing of it by the Spirit for God and His holy will and work. The first, the conversion of the soul, He may do at a distance, or by a momentary act. The baptism of the Spirit is God's residence in the soul, which is a closer union and a more continuous communion and working. The one is the building of a house, and I may build a hundred houses; the other is my residence in the house and the making of that house my home.

What are the effects of this divine incoming and occupancy? Let us trace them briefly as Christ Himself reveals them in His own promise.

Gives reality to our union

1. "On that day (i.e., the day when the Comforter comes) you will realize that I am in my Father, and you are in me, and I am in you" (John 14:20). That is to say, the coming of the Holy Spirit will give reality, vividness and intense consciousness to our union with Jesus Christ. We will not be so conscious that we have received the Spirit as that Jesus is dwelling in our hearts and bringing the Father with Him. We will not believe nor hope, but we will intensely know by the deepest spiritual cognition and consciousness, by an intuition deeper than any emotional impression or feeling, that "He is in us, and we in him," and our life is part of His, and His life is part of ours forever.

Do we not long for this? Does not Jesus sometimes seem far away? Is it not difficult for you to
conceive and grasp His personal reality? Does your
heart not hunger for a keen, sweet, constant sense
of His substantial reality? Will you not cry for the
Holy Spirit to make you know that He is in the
Father, and you in Him, and He in you. It is His
own promise. Hold Him to it, and claim it of Him
this day in all His fullness. This is the deepest need
of your spiritual life, to know Jesus as abiding in
you, to understand the secret, which is "Christ in
you, the hope of glory" (Colossians 1:27b); to have
no doubt of it, no vague reaching out for it, but a
deep abiding rest in His abiding love. Claim your
privilege. Blessed Holy Spirit, make Jesus real to
us, and let us know that we are in Him and that He
is in us as never before, in the deep eternal rest,
faith, fellowship and love.

Brings instruction and light

2. The baptism of the Spirit will bring you instruction and light, for He "will teach you all
things" (John 14:26b). Our minds need to be instructed, as well as our spirits united to Christ.
Our thoughts need to be directed in the fullness of
divine truth. Our understanding needs to be illuminated in the knowledge of God and His Word.
Our Bible needs to be made plain and living to us;
and all this the Spirit does. How in a moment He
lights up a passage with a strange vividness, which
we had often read, and which we had intellectually
understood, but had never felt its power! How

plain He makes the subject of sanctification by a single touch of heavenly light! How easy it seems to us to claim Him as a Healer when the truth is brought home to the heart by the Holy Spirit, not as a theory, but as a living light from heaven for our suffering life!

Not only does He teach, but He continues to teach; and He repeats His teaching because He will "remind you of everything I have said to you" (26b). In a moment of perplexity He will suggest to us with strange appropriateness the very thought and word that will bring us direction. In the hour of temptation He will bring to our remembrance the promise that will deliver and overcome the adversary, "the sword of the Spirit, which is the word of God" (Ephesians 6:17b). In the dark night of sorrow He will shed the bright light of His comfort, and the star of promise will shine with a brightness we could not see by day. In time of service He will bring to our remembrance the truth that we need to speak. "He wakens me morning by morning,/ wakens my ear to listen like one being taught" (Isaiah 50:4b), that we may have "an instructed tongue,/ to know the word that sustains the weary" (4a), and "at that time you will be given what to say" (Matthew 10:19b).

As we kneel by the side of the inquirer and the penitent, He will give us the appropriate message. As we meet the assaults and the keen criticism of man, He will enable us to know what we ought to answer every one and will let our speech be always seasoned with grace. And we will often wonder at the strange simplicity and sweetness with which intuitively our thoughts come to us, and someone seems to be thinking in us without our trying. Oh, the blessed help of the Holy Spirit's suggestive ministry! Beloved, do you want this inward monitor, this continual guide, this sweet voice, this whispering presence, this tender mother and guide and friend? Come to Jesus, who baptizes with the Holy Spirit, and receive His richest gift this day.

He will guide

3. He will not only teach, but "he will guide you into all truth" (John 16:13b). This is more than teaching; this is the direction of our steps, the leading of our feet into the paths of Holy will. Wisdom is more than knowledge, and guidance more than instruction. Wisdom is that which shows us where we are and ought to go and keeps us from error and mistake. This is the blessed Spirit's special ministry—to guide the trusting and obedient heart and let it make no mistake, for He "is able to keep you from falling and to present you before his glorious presence without fault and with great joy" (Jude 24). He will show us the way in which we ought to go. He will lead us "on a level path where [we] will not stumble" (Jeremiah 31:9b). Oh, how often we have erred, and how sad the consequences of our mistakes! How our feet have been wounded by the thorns, and our hearts have been pierced by the stings that have followed our disobedience when we knew not why we stumbled! But the

blessed Spirit will give us light and keep us right if we will but trust Him and follow Him and receive Him in His fullness.

Gives success in our work for Him

4. He will give us success in all our work for Him, for "when he comes, he will convict the world of guilt in regard to sin and righteousness and judgment" (John 16:8). We cannot convict men of sin. We may pierce them with a thousand accusings, we may sting them with our reproaches, we may warn them with our solemn messages, we may plead with them with the utmost pathos and tenderness, but we cannot bring conviction to their consciences. But He can. He can make a single word enter the heart like a barbed arrow and slay the pride and self-confidence and lay the sinner in the dust. He can make a single look send Peter down to weep the tender tears that melted but did not break his heart.

And He can convict them of righteousness. He can show them the Savior as their Righteousness, and He can enable the poor sinner, as we point him to Jesus, to "look [at] the Lamb of God, who takes away the sin of the world" (John1:29b), to trust himself in His loving arms, to take Him as his own personal Savior and know that He does save, forgive and sweetly accept forever. He can show the poor, struggling heart God's righteousness, Jesus as the Sanctifier, the Keeper, the Rest. He can enable us to commit our souls to His keeping, and know that what we have entrusted to Him He is able to keep for that day, and so go forward in victory and praise.

He can convict the world of "judgment, because the prince of this world now stands condemned" (16:11). That is, it seems to us He can make the poor, baffled, beaten heart to know that Satan is overcome, that through Jesus he is a conquered foe and that now we need fear him no more but may stand in complete victory and know that neither life, nor death, nor earth, nor hell can ever separate us from the love of Christ.

Gives us power

5. He gives us power. "But you will receive power when the Holy Spirit comes on you" (Acts 1:8a), were the Master's parting words, "and you will be my witnesses." This is not the power of human persuasion or natural ability of any kind, but it is the divine power working through us. It is that which makes our words and acts effectual. It is that strange influence which makes things tell and often brings out of the very little things mighty and lasting results. This made Peter's sermon on the day of Pentecost, although the utterance of a few simple words of truth, the means of converting thousands of souls. This made Paul's ministry mighty through God to the establishment of Christianity in all the world. And this will make the weak things to shame the things that are strong; the things that are despised, the foolish things, the things that are not, to nullify the things that are (1 Corinthians 1:27–28), that the weakness of God

may be stronger than men and the foolishness of God wiser than men; for Christ is the power of God and the wisdom of God through the Holy Spirit.

Gives us courage

6. The Holy Spirit gives us courage. "When they saw the courage of Peter and John . . . they took note that these men had been with Jesus" (Acts 4:13), and so "God did not give us a spirit of timidity" (2 Timothy 1:7a). The Holy Spirit is courage. He makes the heart strong, and sets the face like a flint in the steps of faith and the path of duty and the battle of the Lord. Timid one, do you want to be brave? Fearful one, do you want to be strong? Shrinking one, do you want to stand firm? "Receive the Holy Spirit."

Gives us wisdom

7. He gives us wisdom. This was the endowment of Stephen and his brethren. This was Paul's assurance to Timothy: God has given us the Spirit "of a sound mind" (2 Timothy 1:7b, KJV). It was He who enabled Paul to form his plans and purposes. Especially do we read in the life of Paul that at a certain crisis he purposed in the Spirit that he would adopt a certain plan of work and pursue certain lines in his missionary journey. Although every influence on earth and every power from beneath seemed leagued together to defeat his purpose, and even the very saints of God and the prophets of inspiration tried to turn him aside, that purpose which had been formed "in the

Spirit" was literally fulfilled, and he was held to it with the tenacity of victorious faith. So He will guide our plans, establish our purposes, and accomplish our highest, holiest desires for the glory and work of God.

Gives us love

8. He is the Spirit of love. After the gifts of power referred to in the 12th chapter of First Corinthians, the apostle tells us that the greatest of these is love. It is emphatic, it is important to notice that the terms in which this is spoken of distinctly imply that it is not a human virtue or the exercise of any will of our own or any feeling of our natural heart, but it is a distinct and supernatural gift of the Spirit.

The word for love is *charitas*, and the word for the gift of grace is *charis*, so that it is distinctly recognized as a divine gift and not in any sense a personal quality. He will give us this wondrous love in all its fullness, sweetness and victorious power.

Would you have the love that suffers long and is kind? Receive the Holy Spirit. Would you have the love that envies not and does not boast, but acts ever with sweet and lowly meekness? Receive the Holy Spirit.

Would you have the love that does not behave in pride and cannot do a rude act or speak a hard and harmful word? Receive the Holy Spirit.

Would you have the love that is not self-sustaining, but is ever self-forgetful, lives for others and

for God without thinking for itself? Receive the
baptism of the Holy Spirit.

Would you have the love that thinks no evil, that
allows no thought of suspicion ever to touch you,
that imagines no wrong in a brother, that would
rather be deceived than think evil, that believes all
things with simple, artless confidence, that hopes
all things, even though the present seems all
wrong, and covers the future with faith and prayer
and blessing even for the unworthy heart? Would
you know the rest of being saved from thinking of
your brother's faults and living in a constant atmosphere of sweetest confidence and innocence
and harmlessness like a little nestling dove?

Receive from Jesus His greatest gift. Receive
from the Spirit His richest, His highest grace, the
grace of heavenly love. Would you have the love
that never fails, that will never again pierce your
heart with a thorn, never again sting you with that
with which you stung your brother? Come to Him
who baptizes with the Holy Spirit and let Him put
into you the same Spirit that made Him holy,
harmless, undefiled and separate from sinners, the
Christ of love.

Gives victory in temptation

9. He is the Spirit that shields you from temptation and gives you victory in the hour of conflict.
"For he will come like a pent-up flood/ that the
breath of the Lord drives along" (Isaiah 59:19b).
He will so fill you with His own presence that the
shafts will not stick, but He in you will resist, repel

and hurl back all the wild billows of the adversary's rage. Like the red-hot iron that repels the slightest particle of water or dust from adhering to it because of its heat, so the kindled Spirit will throw off the touches of the enemy. You will move on in glory and victory, and He will be a wall of fire around you and the glory in the midst.

The Spirit of prayer

10. He is the Spirit of prayer, for "the Spirit himself intercedes for us with groans that words cannot express" (Romans 8:26b). This is our highest service for God; and they who are ever filled with the Spirit will be able to touch the throne with the very power of God, and the prayer that rises from your heart will be a divine power, and He will know instinctively that it has the answer even before it asks because it is the thought and will of God reflected back again to Him from whom it came. Would you have the power that will move heaven and earth, that will prevail with God and man, that will take the fullness of Christ's promises for these last days, that will meet the mighty conflicts that are coming in victorious omnipotence? Come to Him who baptizes with the Holy Spirit and be endued with power from on high.

We are in the days of supernatural conflict; we are touching the borders of the tribulation times. We are feeling the dragon-wing that is in a little while to overshadow the earth and blot out the very light of the sun. We are nearing these dark hours from which Christ is to call up His own elect. Deeper, stronger, subtler than ever before, more penetrating, more mighty are the weapons that are against us and the forms that assail and resist us. We must be encased in the armor of fire. We must be filled with the living God. We must be baptized with the Holy Spirit and baptized as we never have been before with the all-encompassing presence of God, where no joint in the harness can let in an arrow of the enemy and no slip for a single second gives him the slightest advantage. Oh! Thou who baptizes with the Holy Spirit, hear Thy people's prayer, robe them in Thine own omnipotence, clothe them in the garments of Thy fire, baptize them with the fullness of the seven-fold Holy Spirit, and keep them abiding in Thee and walking in the Spirit every breath and every step.

The Spirit of hope

11. He is the Spirit of hope. "May the God of hope fill you with all joy and peace as you trust in him, so that you may overflow with hope by the power of the Holy Spirit" (Romans 15:13). He, and He alone, can take the fears out of your heart and the shadows from your future. He can thrust away the dark clouds of dread that blot out all light and confidence and that cover everything with the dismal shadow of despair. He can illuminate your own path through life with sweet and heavenly confidence. He can unfold to you the vision of the land that is very far off. He can show the stretches of the outreaching of God's blessed promises for you and

all His glorious work for you. Yes, He can show you the coming of the King in His glory and even touch your heart with the thrill of personal hope and the expectation of beholding Him with these mortal eyes and preparing this world for His glorious advent.

What is implied in receiving this baptism?

1. The very thought of baptism suggests the deeply solemn thought of death and resurrection. Baptism is burial and a new life; and, therefore, to receive the fullness of the Holy Spirit there must be death—the death of all that will and can die, for only that which is imperishable ought to live. The gold cannot be burned, therefore you need not fear to die in the arms of Jesus to everything that is capable of dying. Everything that will not die is safe, for only that which is divine can stand the fire of God. Yield yourself unto His death in all the fullness of His thought and then rise into life in all the fullness of His will and be baptized into the Spirit. Therefore you that have died to self and earth have received, and will receive in that measure the fullness of His Spirit and life, even in those very places where you have most truly died. And you that have not received the fullness of His baptism are, perhaps, hindered because in some place you have not died with your Lord, or having died, have not risen again as well as to die, and the voice of heaven, which says, "Arise, shine, for your light has come,/ and the glory of the LORD rises upon you" (Isaiah 60:1).

2. The term baptism suggests great fullness. It is

into an ocean that you are baptized. It is not a sprinkled drop, but it is a great unfathomable sea, and God is calling us to go out into the depths of Himself. Too long we stayed in the shallow surf, swept by its surges, defiled by its miry waters and beaten by its mighty breaker. Out beyond are the depths of calm, the fullness unfathomable. Launch out into the deep, out into the fullness of God.

3. This figure suggests great simplicity of receiving the Holy Spirit. It is easy to be baptized. You have just to let yourself go and sink into the floods or lie restfully in the hand that upholds you or on the bosom of the wave whereon you repose. So it is a very simple thing to receive the Holy Spirit. It is trust. How little we trust the Spirit! How we strive after some deep filling when in quietness and restfulness we might receive His heavenly life and influence.

The rock of Kadesh was the type of the Holy Spirit's deeper overflowing. The command to Moses was to speak to the rock, but on no account to strike it; so his striking the rock became a sin and offense, which did not hinder the water coming, but hindered his full blessing.

There is something very suggestive in this simple thought of speaking to the rock. It is the attitude of simple trust and confidence and quietness. Speak to the rock. Draw near in the desert, amid the hot and burning sands, thirsty, weary, fainting, everything around us wretched and sad. The face of yonder rock seems hard as flint, but in its bosom are stores of infinite refreshing.

It needs no violent grasp, no voice, nor touch to bring them forth. Speak the word of simple trust. Speak to the rock, and lo! the waters will gush forth in streams of refreshing, and you will drink, and you will wash in their cool tides until the wilderness and the solitary place will be glad, and the desert will blossom as the rose. It is Jesus who is that Rock. He is standing before you now. He that baptizes you with the Holy Spirit loves you, has redeemed you, will never fail if you will trust Him. Trust Him for the Holy Spirit, and sweetly receive His infinite fullness that you may have to give to a thirsty world the fullness which He has given you.

> Fainting in the desert, Israel's thousand stand
> At the rock of Kadesh, hark! the Lord's
>   command,
> Speak to the rock, bid the waters flow,
> Strike not its bosom, opened long ago,
> Speak to the rock 'till the waters flow.
>
> Blessed Rock of Ages, thou art open still
> Blessed Holy Spirit all our being fill;
> Still thou dost say, wherefore struggle so?
> Call to the Spirit, whisper soft and low,
> Speak to the rock, bid the waters flow.
>
> Oh, for trust most simple, fully to believe,
> Oh, for hearts more childlike, freely to
>   receive;
> E'en as a babe, on its mother's breast,

So, on thy bosom let my spirit rest,
Filled with thy life, with thy blessing blest.

Speak to the rock, bid the waters flow,
Doubt not the Spirit, given long ago;
Take what He waiteth, freely to bestow,
Drink 'till its fullness all thy being know.

Christ the Living Vine

I am the vine; you are the branches. If a man remains in me and I in him, he will bear much fruit; apart from me you can do nothing. (John 15:5)

The vine is the most important production of the vegetable creation; therefore it has been used by the devil for greater harm than anything that God ever made, for Satan ever loves to steal God's best gifts. God has always used the vine as the symbol of the most sacred things, its juice being the type of Christ's blood and its stems and branches the most perfect figure of the mystery of godliness, Christ's union with His people. The Scriptures give us no profounder view of Christian life than these verses in John 15 contain. Let us look first at the spiritual teaching and then at some illustrations of this in the figure itself.

The first truth conveyed in the Master's teaching is that of union with Jesus. There are two sides to this. The first is "in me," the second, "I in him."

The first expresses our justification; the second our deeper union with Christ in sanctification. To be in Christ is to accept Him as our Savior and to be justified through His blood and righteousness, accepted by the Father for His sake and received into all His rights and privileges as the children of God and the redeemed family of Christ. There are two races: the Adam race and the Christ race. We are all born in Adam, and in Adam all die, but all who are in Christ will be made alive. And so we came into Christ by receiving Him as our Head and our Savior and being born again into His life through His Holy Spirit. Every believer is in Christ, and there is no condemnation to them that are in Christ Jesus, for we are made accepted in the Beloved.

To be in Christ has reference rather to our standing than actual experience. It denotes the relationship between us and Christ rather than the actual life and realization of His presence and communion. Of course, it will bring an actual experience; but that is more fully described by the other phrase, "I in him." This is the other side of our union with Jesus. It is that which brings Him personally into actual touch with us, for this is the great mystery of redemption, that Christ actually comes to dwell in the heart that is in Him, making it His personal residence and chosen home and filling it with His love and joy and purity.

In the previous chapter He had already explained this union and declared that it would be the first result of the Holy Spirit's coming into the heart, that He should reveal it, consummate it and make it intensely real to our consciousness. "On that day," He says (the day of the Holy Spirit's coming to abide with us), "you will realize that I am in my Father, and you are in me, and I am in you" (John 14:20). And still later He added, "Whoever has my commands and obeys them, he is the one who loves me. He who loves me will be loved by my Father, and I too will love him and show myself to him" (21). And then He adds still further, "My Father will love him, and we will come to him and make our home with him" (23). This is the glorious reality to which He refers in this figure, "I in him."

Again and again it is unfolded in the later teachings of the New Testament. The apostle declares that it was his great mission to unfold it: "the mystery that has been kept hidden for ages and generations . . . which is Christ in you, the hope of glory" (Colossians 1:26–27). It is the last appeal of the ascended Lord to the churches in Asia, that they will open the door and let Him come in and dine with them and they with Him. It is the last thought in His own intercessory prayer as He commits His dear disciples to His Father's keeping, and prays that "the love you have for me may be in them and that I myself may be in them" (John 17:26). It is the secret of peace; for He says, "My peace I give you" (14:27b). It is the secret of faith; for the apostle says, "Christ lives in me. The life I live in the body, I live by faith in the Son of God, who loved me and gave himself for me" (Galatians

2:20b). It is the secret of holiness; for "Christ . . . has become for us . . . holiness" (1 Corinthians 1:30b). It is the secret of power; for "I can do everything through him who gives me strength" (Philippians 4:13). It is the secret of all spiritual blessings, for they are all in Christ Jesus. Such then, are the two sides of our union with Christ, He in us, and we in Him. Even as the branch is in the vine, the members are in the body, the Son is in the Father.

Communion

The next truth conveyed here is communion. "Abide in me." We must act according to the fact of our union and keep up the fellowship and mutual relationships involved in this union. When the wife is married it is expected that she will act accordingly and maintain the attitude of a wife by fellowship and dependence. When a partnership is formed between two human beings, they are expected to cooperate according to the agreement. When the soul and Christ become united, there are certain actual relationships and mutual fellowships which are to be constantly maintained. This is spoken of as abiding, and upon the steadiness and simplicity of this depend the happiness and power of our Christian life.

One of the attitudes implied in abiding is dependence. It is the habit of continually looking to Christ for everything; for He says, "Apart from me you can do nothing" (John 15:5b). We are to continually distrust ourselves, feel our utter inability to think a right thought and to look to Him in utter helplessness; and yet in trustful reliance for every breath, thought and feeling, taking our life each moment from Him, both for soul and body, bringing every temptation to him, every need, every desire, and living really by Him and on Him, as a babe upon its mother.

Another idea expressed by abiding is fellowship in prayer. There is a near atmosphere of prayer and communion which may be ceaselessly maintained between the soul and the Savior. Its spirit is very subtle, its home is like the Holy of Holies, its atmosphere is pure and fragrant as the inner chamber of the sanctuary. It is sullied by a breath of sin; it is broken by a thought of distrust and disobedience. It is a very close place in the "shelter of the Most High . . . in the shadow of the Almighty" (Psalm 91:1). There it is that we learn to pray without ceasing, and in everything give thanks, and like Enoch, walk with God.

Another thought suggested by abiding is the momentary life. It is not a life of drift and impulse, not a life in which we act on general principles, but a moment by moment dependence upon Christ. It is simply finding that the life that can be maintained for one moment can be equally maintained for innumerable moments. It is just living out the simple word of Paul in Colossians, "As you received Christ Jesus as Lord, continue to live in him" (2:6).

There are certain principles affecting this life of abiding. It is a principle of human nature that a succession of momentary acts repeated for a certain time produces a habit of thought and feeling, which at first is a somewhat labored purpose and requires much vigilance to maintain, but gradually grows into a delightful habit of dependence. And the momentary acts of abiding are so simple that they are like the breathing of the lungs.

Our abiding depends upon our obedience. "If you obey my commands, you will remain in my love" (John 15:10a). We will find ourselves, sometimes, in positions where we cannot touch Christ for help and blessing, and the reason is that there is some obstacle between us and our Lord, some disobedience or sin which must be removed. It is a matter not only of trust, but also of rightness, and we will find that our peace and communion depend upon walking closely with Him and hearkening unto His holy will. It is if His words abide in us that we have the promise, "ask whatever you wish" (7b). He will show us faithfully the disobedience or the cloud and will enable us to put it aside, and then will restore to us the joy of His communion and the fullness of His very Spirit. So let us abide in Him.

The effects of abiding

1. *Cleansing.* "You are already clean because of the word I have spoken to you" (3). This word was spoken in the 13th chapter. It came through the washing of the disciples' feet. And so He still waits to wash our feet from the stains of the way, and except He wash we have no part with Him. We must be cleansed and keep clean in order to maintain our communion.

2. *Fruitfulness.* "If a man remains in me and I in him, he will bear much fruit" (John 15:5b). Fruit is different from effort. The farmer toils in his garden as he prunes and waters the tree and cultivates the ground, but the tree has no toil or effort but the spontaneous freedom sends forth its leaves, its blossoms and its fruits.

And so in the Christian life there is no effort in bearing fruit if we have the life of Christ within us. It springs spontaneously from the full heart, the mother of liberty and love. And the fruit of the Spirit is love, joy, peace, longsuffering and all the sweet graces of Christian life, besides the reproducing of ourselves in the lives and souls we bring to Christ.

3. *Answered prayer.* "If you remain in me and my words remain in you, ask whatever you wish, and it will be given you" (7). The reason for this is our prayer will be His prayer, our desire will be His desire, our thought will be His thought, our faith will be His faith, and we will know as we ask that He accepts and gives because He prompts the prayer as He walks with us.

4. *Love.* "As the Father has loved me, so have I loved you. Now remain in my love" (9). It is a blessed thing to live in love. Some people love in an atmosphere of constant duty. Our privilege is to live in an atmosphere of love, and to be so pervaded with the dear love of Jesus that we will know that He is always pleased with us, though we often make mistakes, yet He accepts our true heart and loves us with all His heart.

5. *Joy.* "I have told you this so that my joy may be in you and that your joy may be complete" (11). If He is in us, His joy will be in us, and our hearts will spring and sing with a gladness not our own, but wholly prompted by His Spirit within us.

6. *Obedience.* "You are my friends if you do what I command" (14). This is not obedience usually, but it is obedience unconditionally and under all circumstances to "what I command" (14).

7. *Friendship.* "You are my friends if you do what I command. I no longer call you servants, because a servant does not know his master's business. Instead, I have called you friends, for everything that I learned from my Father I have made known to you" (14–15). It is delightful to walk with Jesus in holy confidence and know that we have His freest communion and that He treats us as His beloved ones.

8. *Permanence in our work.* "You did not choose me, but I chose you and appointed you to go and bear fruit—fruit that will last" (16a). That which springs from Him will last and will meet us again, not only here, but in the life to come.

These are the blessings of abiding. How precious, how complete, how eternal! Oh, that we may not miss one of them, but live so closely to our Lord that we will have all the good pleasure of His goodness and the fullness of His blessings!

Some illustrations of these truths

1. The vine and the branch are one. The vine is not separate from the branch, but the vine in-

cludes the branch. And so Christ is not the vine separated from us, but the full Christ consists of Christ the Head and us the body. Christ has become forever so identified with us that He needs us to complete Himself. His joy is not complete without us. His glory is fulfilled in our glory and blessing.

2. The branches need much pruning. Much of the gardener's work is to prune down the growth that is excessive and that would simply produce show and not fruit. And so our gentle and gracious Father cuts back much of our life that would simply grow into selfish luxuriance and only leaves that which can bear real fruit unto Him. Let us trust Him. He is not destroying the tree, but only correcting it and its form and enriching its fruitfulness and value.

3. The branches that bear fruit in the vine are the fresh ones. The little shoots that will come forth this spring, they alone bear the fruit. The old dried branches bear no fruit. They support the ones that do. And so there must be constant freshness and growth to our spiritual life if there is to be fruit. Only that which God is really doing in you, and doing today, will bear fruit to others. You cannot take the experience of a year ago and serve the Lord with that. You must know Christ today in fresh and ceaseless communion, or you cannot accomplish any effective work for Him.

4. The vine is of no use for anything else but for fruit. It cannot be made into lumber or furniture; it has but one purpose. And so the Christian, espe-

cially the consecrated Christian, is worthless and useless unless he abides in Christ and bears fruit for God. Oh, that we may continually abide and bear much fruit, for "this is to my Father's glory, that you bear much fruit" (8a), and thus the Son will be satisfied for the travail of His soul and the sacrifice of His life.

Books by A.B. Simpson

The Best of A.B. Simpson
        (compiled by Keith M. Bailey)
The Christ in the Bible Commentary—Six Volumes
Christ in the Tabernacle
Christ in You
The Christ of the Forty Days
The Cross of Christ
Danger Lines in the Deeper Life
Days of Heaven on Earth (devotional)
Divine Emblems
The Fourfold Gospel
The Gospel of Healing
The Holy Spirit—Power from on High
In Step with the Spirit
The Land of Promise
                (commentary on the Song of Songs)
A Larger Christian Life
The Life of Prayer
The Lord for the Body
Loving As Jesus Loves
Missionary Messages
The Names of Jesus
Portraits of the Spirit-filled Personality
Practical Christianity
Seeing the Invisible
Serving the King
The Spirit-filled Church in Action
The Supernatural
Walking in Love
When God Steps In
When the Comforter Came

Wholly Sanctified
The Word Made Flesh
    (commentary on the Gospel of John)

Booklets by A.B. Simpson

A.W. Tozer and A.B. Simpson on Spiritual Warfare
Called to Serve at Home
Christ Our Sanctifier: Reflections on the Deeper Life
Gifts and Grace
Hard Places: Stepping Stones to Spiritual Growth
Higher and Deeper: A Roadmap for Christian Maturity
Himself
Is Life Worth Living? A Study in Ecclesiastes
Paul: Ideal Man, Model Missionary
Thirty-One Kings: Victory over Self
Women in Ministry

Books about A.B. Simpson

All for Jesus (History of The Christian and
    Missionary Alliance) by Robert Niklaus et al
*The Baptism of the Holy Spirit: The Views of A.B.
    Simpson and His Contemporaries* by Richard
    Gilbertson
The Birth of a Vision, edited by David F. Hartzfeld
    and Charles Nienkirchen
*Body and Soul: Evangelism and the Social Concern of
    A.B. Simpson* by Daniel J. Evearitt